CARRIER STRIKE

A Photo History of Aircraft Carriers in World War II

Donald Nijboer

STACKPOLE
BOOKS

Essex, Connecticut
Blue Ridge Summit, Pennsylvania

STACKPOLE BOOKS

An imprint of Globe Pequot, the trade division of
The Rowman & Littlefield Publishing Group, Inc.
4501 Forbes Blvd., Ste. 200
Lanham, MD 20706
www.rowman.com

Distributed by NATIONAL BOOK NETWORK

Copyright © 2023 by Donald Nijboer

All rights reserved. No part of this book may be reproduced in any form or by any electronic or mechanical means, including information storage and retrieval systems, without written permission from the publisher, except by a reviewer who may quote passages in a review.

British Library Cataloguing in Publication Information available

Library of Congress Cataloging-in-Publication Data

ISBN 978-0-8117-7294-5 (paperback)
ISBN 978-0-8117-7295-2 (electronic)

∞™ The paper used in this publication meets the minimum requirements of American National Standard for Information Sciences—Permanence of Paper for Printed Library Materials, ANSI/NISO Z39.48-1992.

CONTENTS

Chapter 1 U.S. Navy Carriers 1
Chapter 2 British Royal Navy Aircraft Carriers 59
Chapter 3 German, French, and Italian Aircraft Carriers. 105
Chapter 4 Japanese Aircraft Carriers. 113

    About the Author 164

CHAPTER 1

U.S. NAVY CARRIERS

American battleships during fleet maneuvers, September 1940. A mixed formation of carrier monoplane and biplane fighters, torpedo bombers, and dive-bombers pass over the fleet. In just a few short years, the ascendancy of the aircraft carrier over the battleship as the main fighting unit in the major navies around the world would be complete. (U.S. Naval Historical Center)

The USS *Langley* (CV-1), 1922, was adopted from the collier, USS *Jupiter*. It was the U.S. Navy's first aircraft carrier and could carry thirty-four aircraft. Early carrier aircraft lacked the range and payload to be truly effective against battleships and heavy cruisers. (U.S. Naval Historical Center)

USS *Lexington* launching Martin T4M-1 torpedo planes. The *Lexington* (CV-2) and sister ship, *Saratoga* (CV-3), were built from existing cruiser hulls. When commissioned in 1927, they were the largest carriers in service and would remain so until the advent of the Japanese carrier *Shinano* in 1944. (U.S. Naval Historical Center)

U.S. Navy Carriers

USS *Ranger* (CV-4). *Ranger* was the first U.S. carrier built from the keel up. Ranger was designed to carry seventy-six aircraft. Original armament consisted of eight 5-inch/.38-cal guns and forty .50-cal machine guns. (U.S. Naval Historical Center)

This vertical aerial photograph from 17,200 feet taken on May 3, 1940, shows how vast Pearl Harbor really was. There are eight battleships and the carrier *Yorktown* (CV-5) tied up along the island's southeastern side (toward the top), with two more battleships alongside 1010 dock at top right center. Two light cruisers and two destroyers are among the ships moored along Ford Island's northwestern side. Seventeen other cruisers and more than thirty destroyers are also visible, mainly in East Loch. (U.S. Naval Historical Center)

USS *Enterprise* (CV-4) docked at Ford Island, Pearl Harbor, March 1942. This view of the aft end of the island clearly shows the heavy deck crane, two 1.1-inch gun mounts, and three large circular loudspeakers. These speakers were critical for the transmission of instructions for both deck and flight crew across a windswept, noisy flight deck. (U.S. Naval Historical Center)

Facing page bottom: Just eight weeks after the Pearl Harbor attack, U.S. carrier strikes were mounted against Japanese targets in the Pacific. On February 24, aircraft from the *Enterprise* (CV-6) struck Wake Island. After finishing its bomb run, a Douglas TBD-1 Devastator flies over the island. Note fires burning in the lower center. (U.S. Naval Historical Center)

Japanese attack on Pearl Harbor, December 7, 1941. This panorama view of the raid shows antiaircraft shell bursting overhead. The photograph looks southwesterly from the hills behind the harbor. Large column of smoke in lower right center is from the burning USS *Arizona* (BB-39). Smoke somewhat further to the left is from the destroyers *Shaw* (DD-373), *Cassin* (DD-372), and *Downes* (DD-375), in drydocks at the Pearl Harbor Navy Yard. (U.S. Naval Historical Center)

USS *Lexington* (CV-2) under Japanese dive-bomber attack, shortly before noon, May 8, 1942, during the Battle of the Coral Sea. After being hit by two torpedoes and two bombs, the *Lexington* suffered several internal explosions, causing major damage. At 7:52 p.m. torpedoes from the destroyer USS *Phelps* sent the *Lexington* to the bottom. (U.S. Naval Historical Center)

Lexington burning and sinking after her crew abandoned ship during the Battle of the Coral Sea. Note planes parked aft, where fires have not yet reached. (U.S. Naval Historical Center)

USAAF aircrewmen preparing .50-cal machine-gun ammunition on the flight deck of the USS *Hornet* (CV-8) while the carrier was steaming toward the mission's launching point. Three of their B-25B bombers are visible. In one of the most audacious carrier strikes of the war, the U.S. Navy launched sixteen USAAF B-25 medium bombers off the coast of Japan on April 18. Each aircraft was armed with a single 500-pound bomb and incendiary cluster. Known as the Doolittle Raid, the attack came as complete surprise and was a devastating shock to the Japanese.

Douglas SBD-3 Dauntless scout bombers of VS-5 preparing to take off from the USS *Yorktown* during operations in the Coral Sea, April 1942. (U.S. Naval Historical Center)

Along with the Douglas SBD Dauntless, the Vought SB2U Vindicator was the other U.S. Navy dive-bomber in service at the beginning of the war. Here SB2Us of VS-41 and VS-42 and a Grumman F4F Wildcat prepare for an antisubmarine patrol onboard the USS *Ranger*, November 1941. (U.S. Naval Historical Center)

Douglas TBD-1 Devastators of Torpedo Squadron 8 prepare for takeoff on *Enterprise*'s flight deck on the morning of June 4, 1942. Only three of these aircraft would survive their part in the epic Battle of Midway and return to the *Enterprise*. (Author's Collection)

After dropping their torpedoes, two B5N2 "Kates" pass the *Yorktown* surrounded by exploding AA fire. Moments later two torpedoes hit the *Yorktown* with devastating results. During the war, torpedoes were the true ship killers, and every time a U.S. carrier was hit by a torpedo (either air dropped or from a submarine), it either sank or was severely damaged. (U.S. Naval Historical Center)

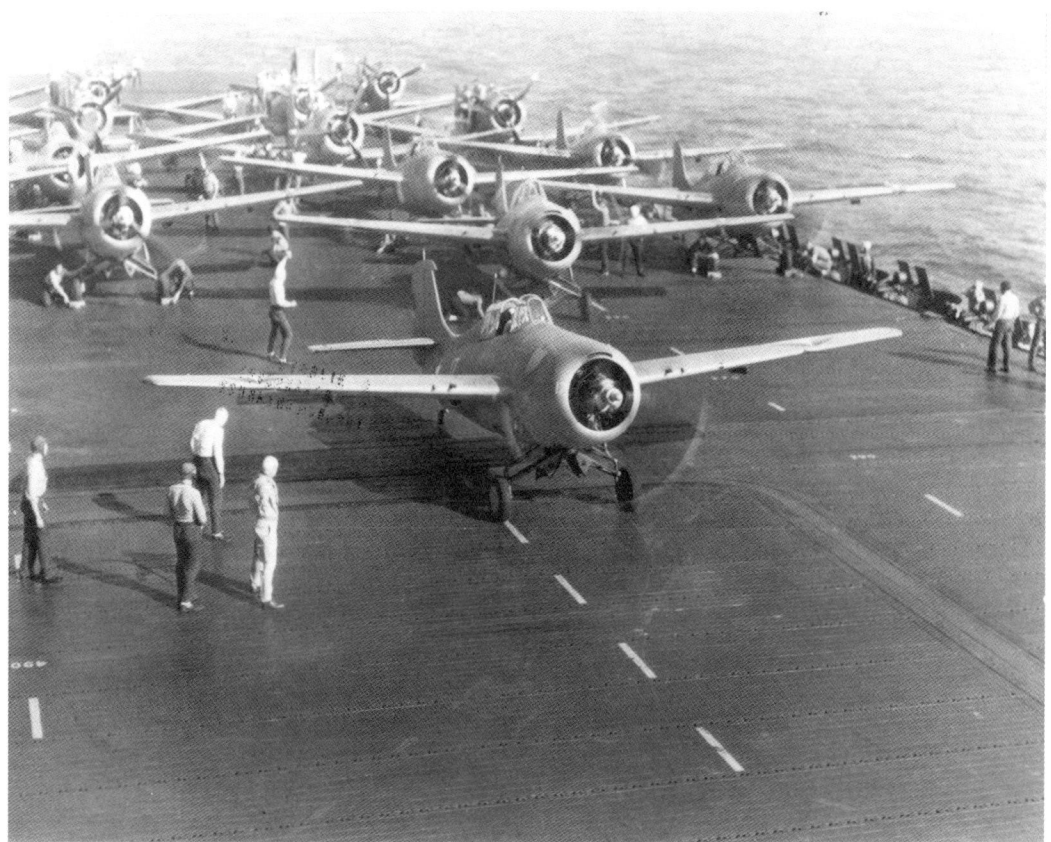

F4F-3 Wildcats from VF-6 take off from the *Enterprise*, May 12, 1942. The F4F-3 was armed with four .50-cal machine guns and had a maximum speed of 335mph. (Author's Collection)

Grumman F4F-3 Wildcat VF-3White-5 from the USS *Yorktown* lands on the CV-8 USS *Hornet* June 4, 1942, during the Battle of Midway. By June, most F4F-3s were replaced by the F4F-4 version with folding wings and six .50-cal machine guns. In *Yorktown*'s after-action report, pilots were not enamored of the new mounts: "The fighter pilots are very disappointed with the performance and length of sustained fire power of the F4F-4 airplanes. The Zero fighters could easily outmaneuver and outclimb the F4F-3, and the consensus of fighter pilot opinion is that the F4F-4 is even more sluggish and slow than the F4F-3. It is also felt that it was a mistake to put 6 guns on the F4F-4 and thus to reduce the rounds per gun. For the opposition now being encountered the combination of 4 guns and 450 rounds per gun is much superior to the 6 guns with 240 rounds per gun." (NARA)

SBD-3 Dauntless of VB-6 preparing for takeoff on the USS *Enterprise* (CV-6). Air group commander Lt. Cmdr. Howard Young, USN, is in the following plane, as denoted by the letters "GC" (Group Commander) on the cowl front. Note the gun gallery of .50-cal water-cooled Brownings. *Enterprise* was armed with up to twenty-four .50-cal machine guns for defense against dive-bombers. (U.S. Naval Historical Center)

USS *Wasp* (CV-7) burning and sinking, south of San Cristobal Island. Torpedoed by a Japanese submarine on September 15, 1942, the *Wasp* was hit three times. With the crew unable to contain the damage, the carrier was finally sent to the bottom by three torpedoes from the destroyer *Lansdowne*. (U.S. Naval Historical Center)

A Japanese "Val" dive-bomber trails smoke as it dives toward the USS *Hornet* (CV-8) on the morning of October 16, 1942, during the Battle of Santa Cruz. This plane struck the ship's stack and then her flight deck. A B5N2 "Kate" is flying over the *Hornet* after dropping its torpedo, and another Val is off the bow. Note the 5-inch AA shell bursting between the *Hornet* and the camera, spraying the sea with shrapnel. (U.S. Naval Historical Center)

A Grumman F4F-4 Wildcat fighter taking off from the USS *Ranger* (CV-4) to attack targets ashore during the invasion of Morocco, November 8, 1942. Note the Army observation planes in the left middle distance. (U.S. Naval Historical Center)

U.S. and British escort carriers played a critical role in all theaters of war. Not only did they provide convoy escort and air-to-ground support for marines and army units ashore, but they also transported large numbers of aircraft ready to fight. During the Marianas Operation, June 1944, these USAAF P-47D fighters of the 73rd Fighter Squadron, Seventh Air Force, are launched from the USS *Manila Bay* (CVE-61) for delivery to airfields on Saipan, June 24, 1944. For these army pilots, it would be their first and last catapult launch from an aircraft carrier. (U.S. Naval Historical Center)

F4F-3 Wildcats of VF-41 on the USS *Ranger* (CV-4) in 1942. These F4F-3s are armed with two 100-pound bombs for antisubmarine patrol. (U.S. Naval Historical Center)

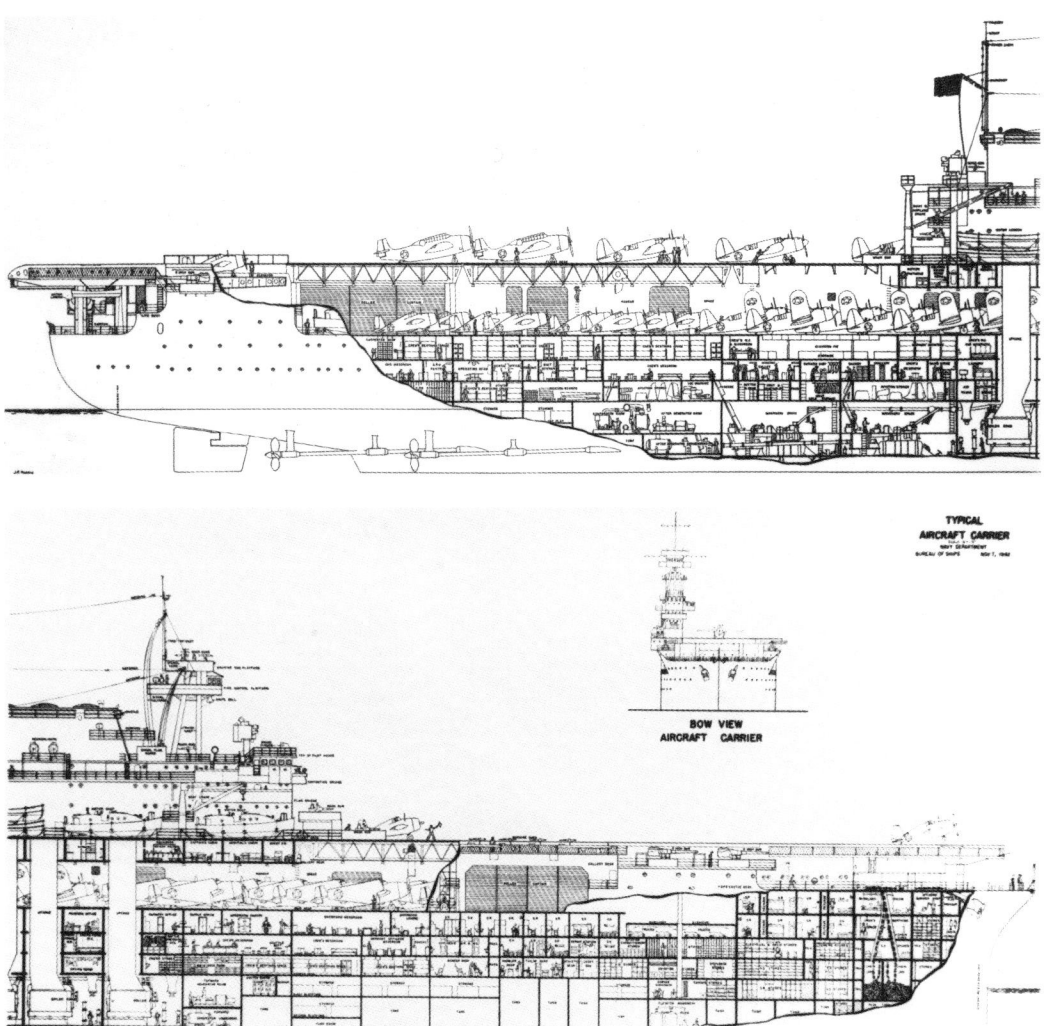

Typical aircraft carrier cutaway profile drawing prepared by the Bureau of Ships, November 7, 1942. Ship shown represents the USS *Yorktown* (CV-5) and USS *Enterprise* (CV-6), combining features of the ships' peacetime and early wartime configurations. (U.S. Naval Historical Center)

The Americans knew the coming war with Japan would be a long one, and early defeats would be inevitable. Well before the attack on Pearl Harbor, the U.S. Navy was already drawing up plans for new fast, powerful aircraft carriers. The first new carrier in the class was the *Essex* (CV-9) as part of the Naval Expansion Act of 1938. In June 1940, three more were ordered, and after the fall of France to German forces, seven more were added to the list. Here the *Essex* is underway in May 1943. On deck are twenty-four SBDs, eleven F6F Hellcats, and eighteen TBF Avengers. (U.S. Naval Historical Center)

U.S. Navy Carriers

The USS *Independence* (CVL-22) light carrier in San Francisco Bay, California, on July 15, 1943. On deck are nine SBD dive-bombers and nine TBM Avenger torpedo bombers. The non-folding wings of the SBD meant that fewer aircraft could be carried, thus reducing the carrier's effectiveness. (U.S. Naval Historical Center)

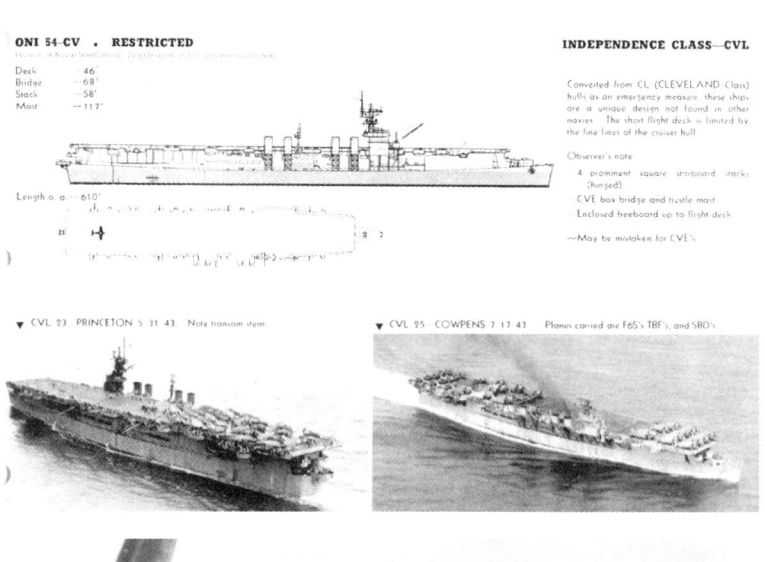

The Independence-class light carrier was a ship the navy did not want. U.S. President Roosevelt knew that large carriers such as the new Essex class would not be ready until mid- to late 1943. To bridge the gap, the president suggested using cruiser hulls of the Cleveland class to construct a light carrier. The navy disagreed but reluctantly accepted, and by June 1942 the first conversion was ordered. (U.S. Naval Historical Center)

Operating in the vicinity of the Coral Sea, April 1942. Photographed from a TBD-1 torpedo plane that has just taken off from her deck. Other TBD and SBD aircraft are also ready to be launched. An F4F-3 Wildcat fighter is parked on the outrigger just forward of the island. Other ships in the company include a fleet oiler, a destroyer, and a heavy cruiser. (U.S. Naval Historical Center)

U.S. Navy Carriers

With bombs dropped, five SBDs peel off for a strafing attack on a Japanese radio station, Ulalu Island, Truk Atoll, in the strike of April 29–30, 1944. (U.S. Naval Historical Center)

Photographed from the USS *Makin Island* (CVE-93), three escort carriers steam in column through heavy western Pacific seas, probably in the vicinity of Ulithi Atoll after the Iwo Jima campaign, March 10, 1945. Because of their small aircraft complements, escort carriers had to operate in groups to be effective. Each carrier could carry 24–30 aircraft. A total of seventy-seven escort carriers were commissioned into U.S. Navy service during the war. In addition, American shipyards built thirty-eight escort carriers for the Royal Navy. In comparison, the Imperial Japanese Navy built a total of five escort carriers. (U.S. Naval Historical Center)

USS *Lexington* (CV-16). Flight deck operations was dangerous and exhausting work. Here plane handlers rest during a lull in the Battle of the Philippine Sea, June 19, 1944. Planes in the background are Grumman F6F-3 fighters of VF-16. (U.S. Naval Historical Center)

Southern France invasion, August 1944. Invasion convoy steams toward the objective area during mid-August 1944. Seen from the USS *Tulagi* (CVE-72), the convoy includes three other escort carriers and a large number of merchant ships. The Grumman F6F Hellcat not only fought in the Pacific theater, but it saw action in the Mediterranean, North Atlantic, and Indian Oceans. (U.S. Naval Historical Center)

The pilot's view of the landing signal officer (LSO). Here the LSO appears to be signaling "cut." "This is a mandatory signal. Pilot cuts throttle immediately. He takes his eyes off the signal officer for the first time and looks at the deck for alignment." (NARA)

Landing a damaged aircraft onto a carrier (*Lexington* CV-16) was fraught with danger. Aircraft performance was unpredictable, and the potential for disaster was great. Returning from a Wake Island strike, a damaged Hellcat makes its final approach. The LSO appears to be signaling to the Hellcat pilot that he is "too high" for a safe landing. A go-around in a damaged aircraft often meant ditching or loss of control and crashing into the sea. (U.S. Naval Historical Center)

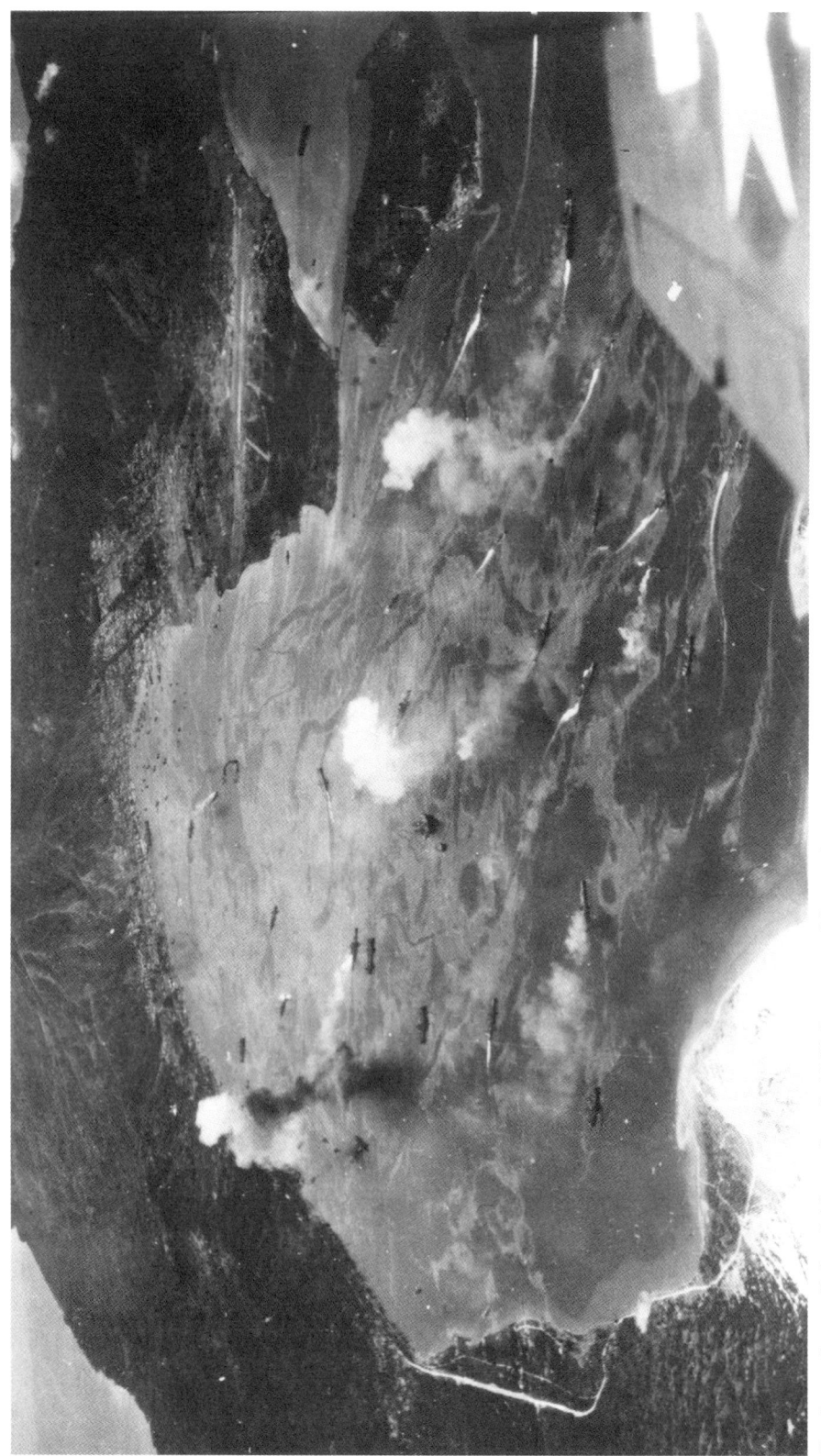

Carrier strike on Rabaul, November 5, 1943. Japanese ships under carrier attack in Simpson Harbor. On the left the cruiser *Maya* is hit, causing a big fire. Several other cruisers are among the ships heading for the open sea, to the right. In the last four months of 1943, U.S. Navy carrier Task Groups operated with impunity, striking Japanese bases at will with few losses. (NARA)

U.S. Navy Carriers 27

This dramatic photograph shows an F6F Hellcat from VF-9 strafing the Japanese destroyer *Tachikaze* during Operation Hailstone, the carrier raid on Truk Lagoon, February 16–18, 1944. The raid was a game-changing success with nine U.S. carriers capable of launching five hundred aircraft. Japanese losses amounted to between 250 and 275 aircraft, 14 combat ships, and 32 merchant ships. Task Force 58 losses counted twenty-five aircraft shot down and twenty-six aircrew killed. (NARA)

Battle of the Philippine Sea, June 1944. A VF-1 "top hatter" F6F-3 fighter is launched from the USS *Yorktown* to intercept enemy forces during the "Marianas Turkey Shoot," June 19, 1944. Note the deck crewman holding his chalkboard with last-minute target information for the pilot. (U.S. Naval Historical Center)

Battle of Leyte Gulf, October 1944. Loading drop tanks on SB2Cs aboard the USS *Lexington* (CV-16) before a search mission, October 25, 1944. These drop tanks contained fifty-eight gallons of fuel. The SB2C could carry two tanks, giving it an extra 116 gallons of fuel. (U.S. Naval Historical Center)

Battle of the Sibuyan Sea, October 24, 1944. Japanese battleship *Yamato* is hit by a bomb near her forward 460mm gun turret during attacks by U.S. carrier planes as she transited the Sibuyan Sea. This hit did not produce serious damage. During the war, armor-piercing bombs dropped by dive-bombers on armored battleships did not contribute significantly to their sinking. They did, however, reduce the effectiveness of their antiaircraft defenses and aided in the effectiveness of torpedo bombing attacks. (U.S. Naval Historical Center)

Carrier raid on Rabaul, November 5, 1943. Medical corpsmen and plane handlers removed casualties from the air group commander's TBF, just after it landed on the USS *Saratoga* (CV-3) after being shot up over Rabaul. The gunner, AOM Kenneth Bratton, was wounded in the plane, and Photographer's Mate First Class Paul Barnett was killed while photographing a Japanese Zero fighter making a head-on attack on the TBF. Cdr. Henry H. Caldwell, the pilot, is climbing from his cockpit, after making a one-wheel landing with no flaps, ailerons, or radio. Flak damage to the tailplane can be seen clearly, top left. (U.S. Naval Historical Center)

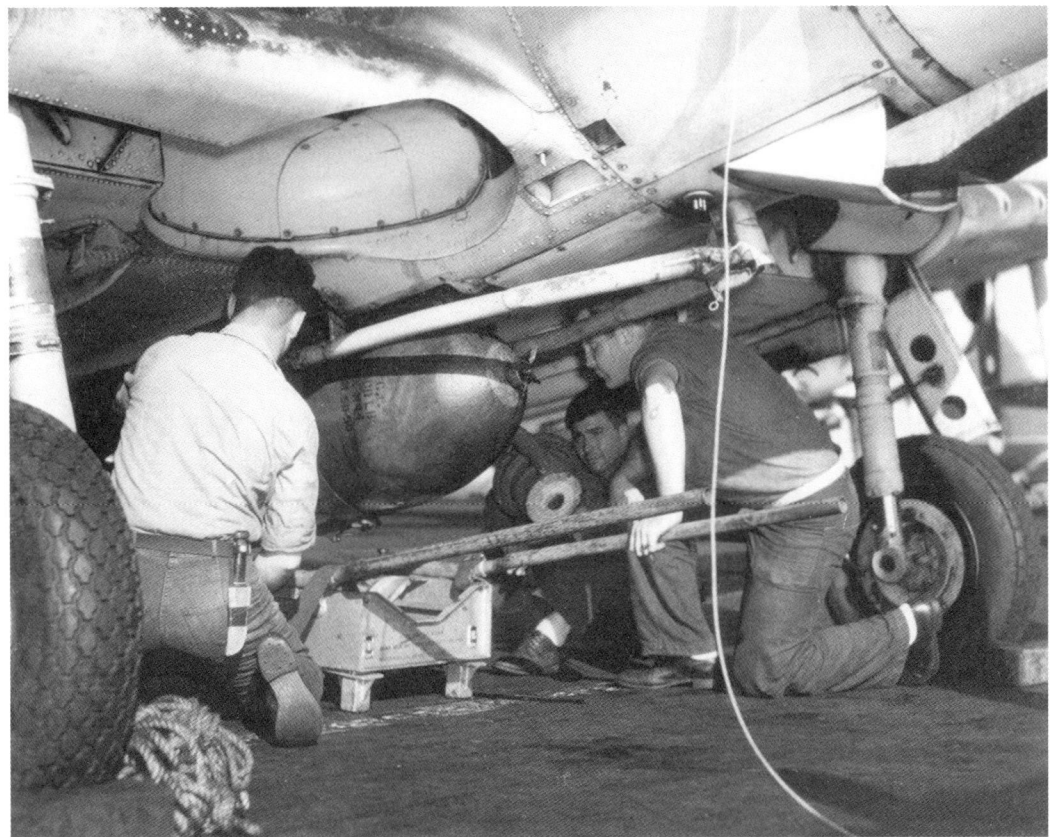

Aviation ordnancemen loading a 1,000-pound general purpose bomb on a Douglas SBD-5 Dauntless diver bomber on board an aircraft carrier, circa 1943–1944. Note landing gear details, bomb cart and crutch, block in the plane's intake, and false gun ports painted on the wing. On a rolling deck this was backbreaking work with little room for error. (U.S. Naval Historical Center)

USS *Cowpens* (CVL-25). Fire was the greatest threat to a ship's survival. Pilot Lt. (Junior Grade) Alfred W. Magee Jr., USNR, evacuates his burning F6F-3 fighter after landing, unaware that it was on fire, during the Gilberts Operation, November 24, 1943. Firefighters rush to the plane and put out the flames in a minute and a half, with no casualties. The fire started as the Hellcat approached the *Cowpens* for an emergency landing. Hellcat Bureau # 66101. (U.S. Naval Historical Center)

USS *Essex* (CV-9). The point of no return. A TBM Avenger, trailing smoke, returns to the carrier after being hit by Japanese antiaircraft fire during the Okinawa Operation, March 28, 1945. Damaged aircraft had one chance to land, either catching a hook or crashing into the crash barrier. (U.S. Naval Historical Center)

The victor and the vanquished. Capture of German Submarine U-505. June 4, 1944, TBM Avenger landing on the USS *Guadalcanal* (CVE-60) while it was towing U-505. The escort carrier kept up flight operations while the captured submarine was being towed toward Bermuda. Of the 758 German U-boats that the Allies sank, escort carriers sank fifty-three and captured one, the U-505. It can be seen today at Chicago's Museum of Science and Industry. (U.S. Naval Historical Center)

Carrier strikes on the Palau Islands. Gunner of the USS *Enterprise* (CV-6) SBD-5 secures equipment as the pilot tries to release the 1,000-pound bomb in preparation for ditching, March 30, 1944. The plane was hit by antiaircraft fire, causing oil to coat the upper fuselage and tail. After ditching, its crew was picked up by a Task Force 58 ship. (U.S. Naval Historical Center)

USS *Princeton* burning soon after being hit by a 1,000-pound bomb from a "Judy" dive bomber while operating off the Philippines on October 24, 1944. The bomb hit started a huge fire in the hanger deck where fuel and torpedoes were being prepared for flight operations. Shortly after, a huge explosion severely damaged the ship, and it was abandoned. A single torpedo from the Destroyer USS *Reno* sent it to the bottom. (U.S. Naval Historical Center)

In these two dramatic photographs a burning Japanese kamikaze "Judy," already hit by AA fire, plunges and hits the USS *Essex* (CV-9) off Luzon, November 25, 1944. (U.S. Naval Historical Center)

The two kamikaze hits on the USS *Bunker Hill* (CV-17) on May 11, 1945, caused extensive damage to both the flight deck and hanger decks. Forced out of the line, the *Bunker Hill* returned to the States for repair. (U.S. Naval Historical Center)

The USS *Hancock* (CV-19) burns in the background after being hit by a single kamikaze as the *Bunker Hill* launches F4U-1Ds. The F4U-1D was best suited to battling the kamikazes, being 30mph faster than the F6F-5 Hellcat. (NARA)

A Japanese Mitsubishi A6M5 Zero attempting a kamikaze attack on the USS *White Plains* (CVE-66) off Leyte, October 25, 1944. Kamikaze aircraft were usually equipped with a single bomb that was to be dropped just prior to the pilot crashing into his target ship. This was the opening salvo of the kamikaze offensive. Its attack demonstrated the difficulty inherent in crashing an aircraft onto a ship. The aircraft missed the ship but hit close aboard along the port side. The shock from the aircraft's exploding bomb was severe enough to force the carrier home for repairs. (U.S. Naval Historical Center)

U.S. Navy Carriers

The industrial might of the United States on full display. The Japanese had no hope of matching America's output of ships, aircraft, and highly trained crews. This photo is titled "Murderers' Row." Third Fleet carriers anchored in Ulithi Atoll, Carolines. Ships are (left to right): USS *Wasp* (CV-18), USS *Yorktown* (CV-10), USS *Hornet* (CV-12), USS *Hancock* (CV-19). A destroyer escort and LCI are passing by. Planes in the foreground on board the USS *Ticonderoga* (CV-14) are F6F Hellcats. (U.S. Naval Historical Center)

With her 5-inch/.38-cal main guns blasting away, the USS *Essex* (CV-9) suffers a near miss on April 15, 1945. Essex-class carriers were the most heavily armed carriers of the war. Long-range guns consisted of twelve 5-inch/.38-cal guns with eight guns mounted in four twin turrets. Range was ten miles with a rate of fire of fifteen rounds a minute. When firing the revolutionary VT fused shell (a warhead with a miniature radar in the nose), it was one of the most effective heavy antiaircraft guns of the war. (U.S. Naval Historical Center)

A close-up of the Camouflage Measure 31-32-33 series, Design 3A on the USS *Hancock* (CV-19). These deceptive camouflage patterns were used to confuse the enemy as to the speed and direction of a ship when spotted. (U.S. Naval Historical Center)

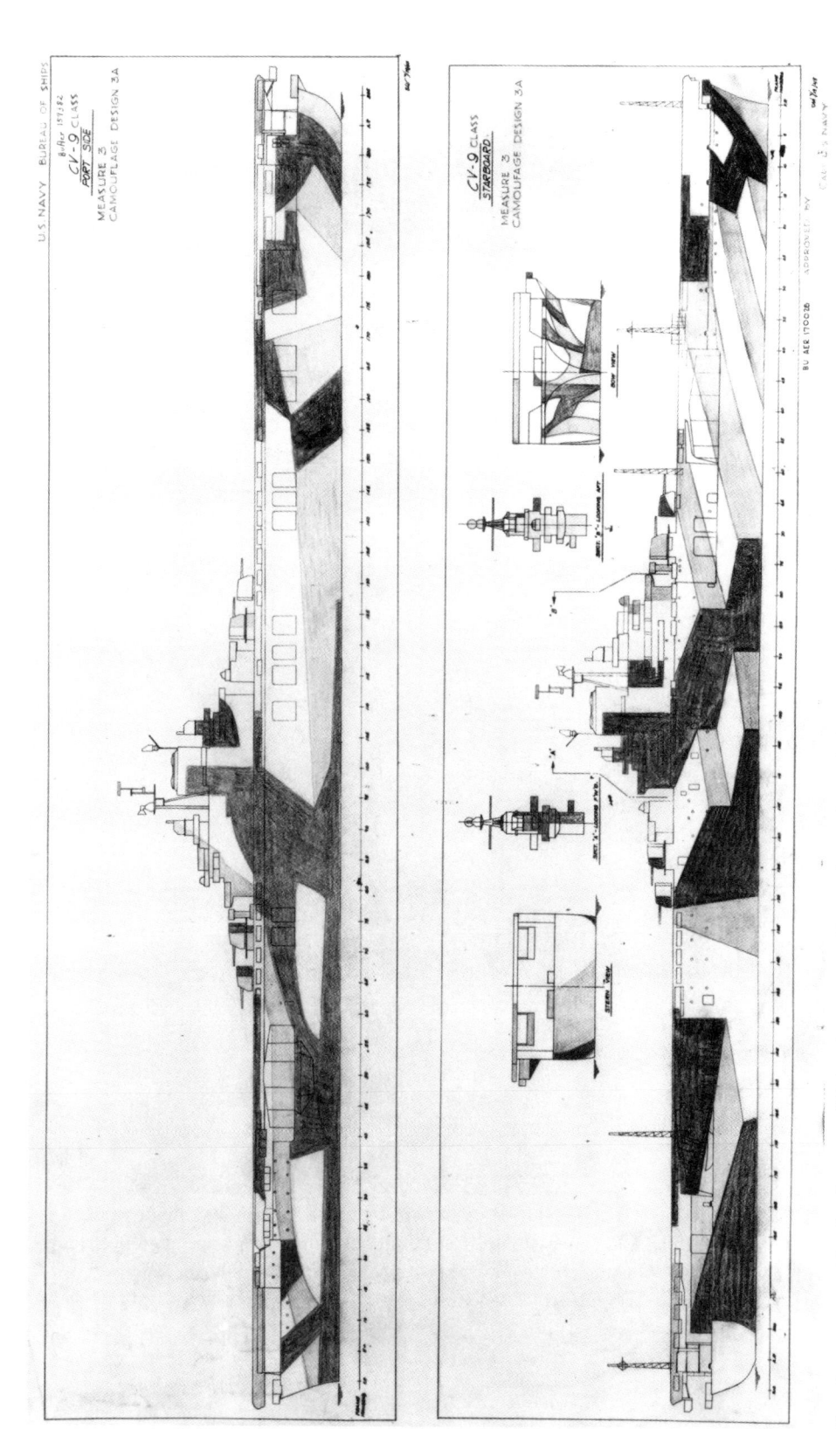

Drawing prepared by the Bureau of Ships for a camouflage scheme intended for aircraft carriers of the CV-9 (Essex) class. This plan, dated July 19, 1943, shows the ship's starboard and port sides, bow, stern, and island ends. The USS *Intrepid* (CV-11), USS *Hancock* (CV-19), and the port side of the USS *Franklin* (CV-13) were painted in this design, using Measure 32 colors (Dull Black, Ocean Gray, and Light Gray). (U.S. Naval Historical Center)

The Japanese battleship *Musashi* is targeted by Helldivers from TG 38.3 during the Battle of the Sibuyan Sea. This was the third raid generated against the super battleship. A fire started by an earlier dive-bombing attack is clearly burning aft, generating significant amounts of smoke. It would take sixteen 1,000-pound bomb hits and fifteen torpedoes to sink the mighty ship. (U.S. Naval Historical Center)

U.S. Navy Carriers

Keeping track of the various U.S. Carrier Task Groups proved difficult for the Japanese. Even when they were able to spot and shadow American carriers, they were often driven off or shot down. The Japanese paid a heavy price. Here an H8K "Emily" flying boat is shot down by Hellcats off Gilbert Island, September 1943. (NARA)

During the battle off Samar, October 25, 1944, the six escort carriers of Taffy 3 were caught by a Japanese task force with four battleships, six heavy cruisers, and smaller escorts. Japanese confusion and poor gunnery, combined with aggressive American actions by the escort carriers' aircraft and their accompanying destroyers and destroyer escorts, saved the task force from complete destruction. *Kitkun Bay* (CVE-71) prepares to launch three FM-2 Wildcat fighters during the battle. Shells from the battleship *Yamato* can be seen splashing near the *White Plains* (CV-66). The Japanese managed to sink just one escort carrier, the *Gambier Bay*. (NARA)

The U.S. Navy proved an unstoppable force beginning in late 1943. Centered on Fast Carrier Task Force, it was a combined-arms weapons system that consisted of modern fleet, light, and escort carriers combined with battleships, cruisers, fleet tankers, and destroyers, tied together by new technologies and tactics and manned by some of the best aviators and sailors in the world. Here Task Group 38.3 (TG 38.3) enters Ulithi Anchorage after strikes against the Japanese on Luzon. In line are the *Langley* (CVL-27), *Ticonderoga* (CV-14), *Washington* (BB-56), *North Carolina* (BB-55), and *South Dakota* (BB-57). (NARA)

Grumman aircraft were tough and designed for adverse carrier operations, but they weren't invincible. Catching the wire didn't always mean a safe landing. This F6F-3 has its tail ripped off after a hard landing aboard the *Belleau Wood*, August 1943. The aircraft plunged over the side, killing the young pilot. (NARA)

U.S. Navy Carriers

In January 1944, the U.S. Fast Carrier Task Force was equipped with its first night fighters, the F4U-2(N). Four were assigned to the USS *Enterprise*. These would be followed by the more numerous Grumman F6F-5(N) Hellcat night fighters seen here fitted with an AN/APS-6 radar. Some were armed with two 20mm M2 cannon in the inner wing bays and four .50-cal machine guns. A total of 1,189 F6F-5N Hellcats had been built by the time production ended in late 1945. (NARA)

A Japanese "Judy" dive-bomber streaks toward the USS *Franklin* (CV-17) during the Battle of the Philippine Sea, June 19, 1944. The *Bunker Hill* would suffer a near miss and managed to shoot down its attacker. (NARA)

The damage by kamikaze attacks could be considerable. After two direct hits by two bomb-laden Zero-sens, the USS *Bunker Hill* (CV-17) was knocked out of the war on May 11, 1945. In this photograph more than twenty Corsairs from VF-84, VMF-221, and VMF-451 were destroyed. The stern elevator is completely wrecked. (NARA)

An SB2C-4E Helldiver of Bombing Squadron (VB) 94 has its engine ripped off in a near-fatal deck crash aboard the USS *Lexington* (CV-16), June 1945. Severely damaged aircraft such as this were beyond the means of repair aboard a carrier. And to clear the deck as quickly as possible, they were simply pushed overboard. (NARA)

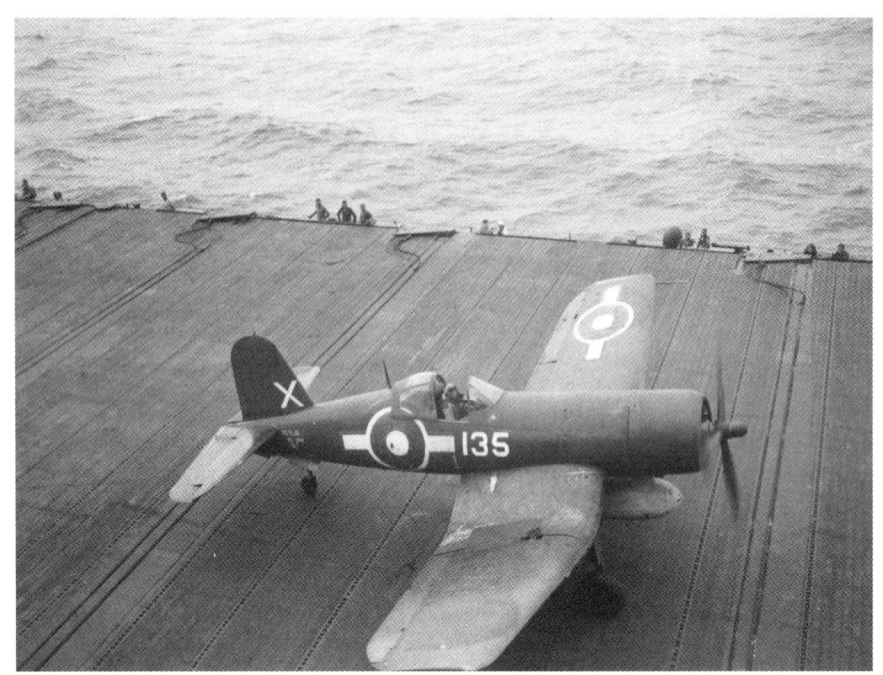

A British Fleet Air Arm Corsair of 1842 NAS off HMS *Formidable* lands aboard the USS *Shangri-La* (CV38), July 1945. British and American carriers never operated in concert. The British Pacific Fleet with its five carriers was given its own targets and assignments. (NARA)

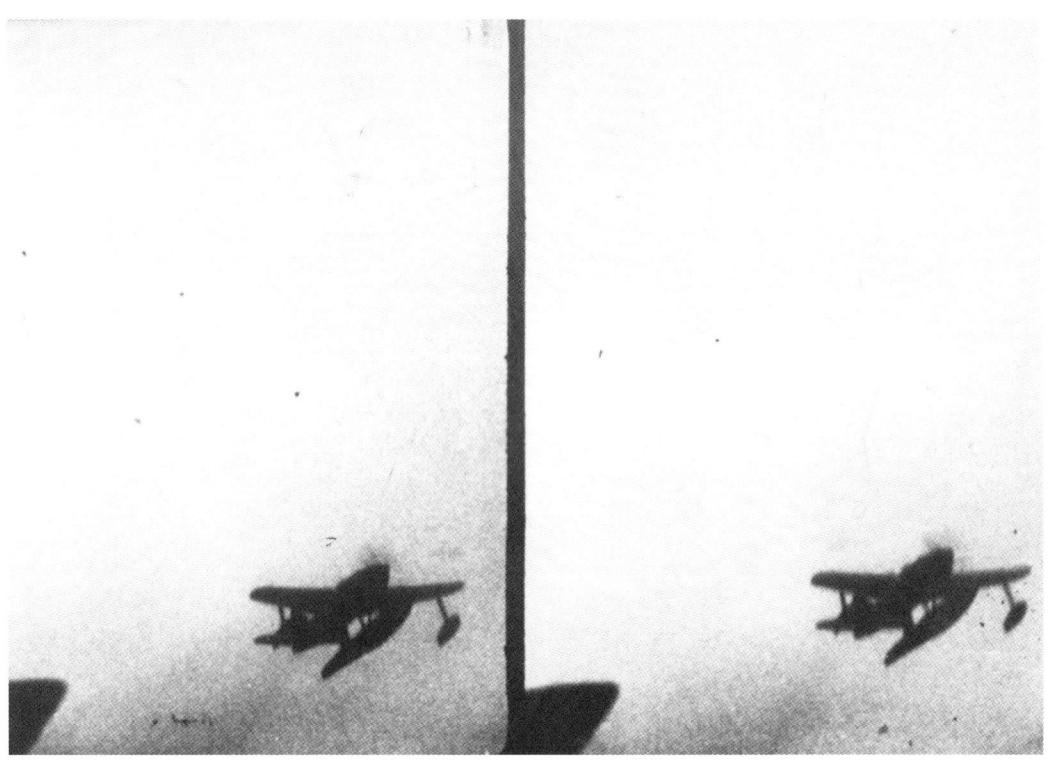

A rare gun camera image of a Kawanishi K1K1 "Rex" floatplane fighter shot down by an F4U Corsair from the *Bunker Hill* during carrier strikes on Kyushu, March 12, 1945. (NARA)

Equipped with a single long-range fuel tank, F4U-1D Corsairs aboard the *Essex* prepare for another airfield strike on the island of Formosa in January 1945. The F4U-1D did away with outboard internal wing fuel tanks, relying instead on the belly-mounted 160-gallon drop tank for a range of 1,051 miles. (NARA)

Napalm bombs appeared late in World War II and proved highly effective against dug-in troops and as an incendiary device. The jellied gasoline, when exploded, ignited fires and would stick to human flesh, causing severe burns and death. This photograph is of the back end of an early napalm bomb showing the rear mount bomb fuse assembly. (NARA)

Air attacks on mainland Japan in 1945 were constant and overwhelming. While the USAAF bombed Japanese cities day and night, carrier aircraft added to the carnage by attacking air bases and naval installations. Here Grumman TBM-3 Avengers and Curtiss SB2C-4 Helldivers from carrier Group 83 from the USS *Essex* (CV-9) salvo their load of 500-pound bombs on Hakodate, July 1945. (NARA)

U.S. Navy Carriers

The remaining Japanese combat vessels in home waters, July 1945, were essentially dead targets. With no fuel or crews to man them, they were no threat to U.S. naval forces. The TF-38 commander, Admiral Cain, raised the issue but was overridden by Admiral Earnest King in Washington. All remaining Japanese warships were to be sunk. Here the Japanese cruiser *Tone* is under attack by carrier aircraft, July 24, 1945. (NARA)

The Japanese IJNAF and IJAAF had no answer to constant air attacks by U.S. carrier aircraft in July and August 1945. Lack of fuel and well-trained pilots meant that the Japanese could only offer a token defense. Here an F6F-5 Hellcat, far right, unleashes its full load of 5-inch air-to-ground rockets toward the burning "Betty" bombers in their revetments, July 1945. (NARA)

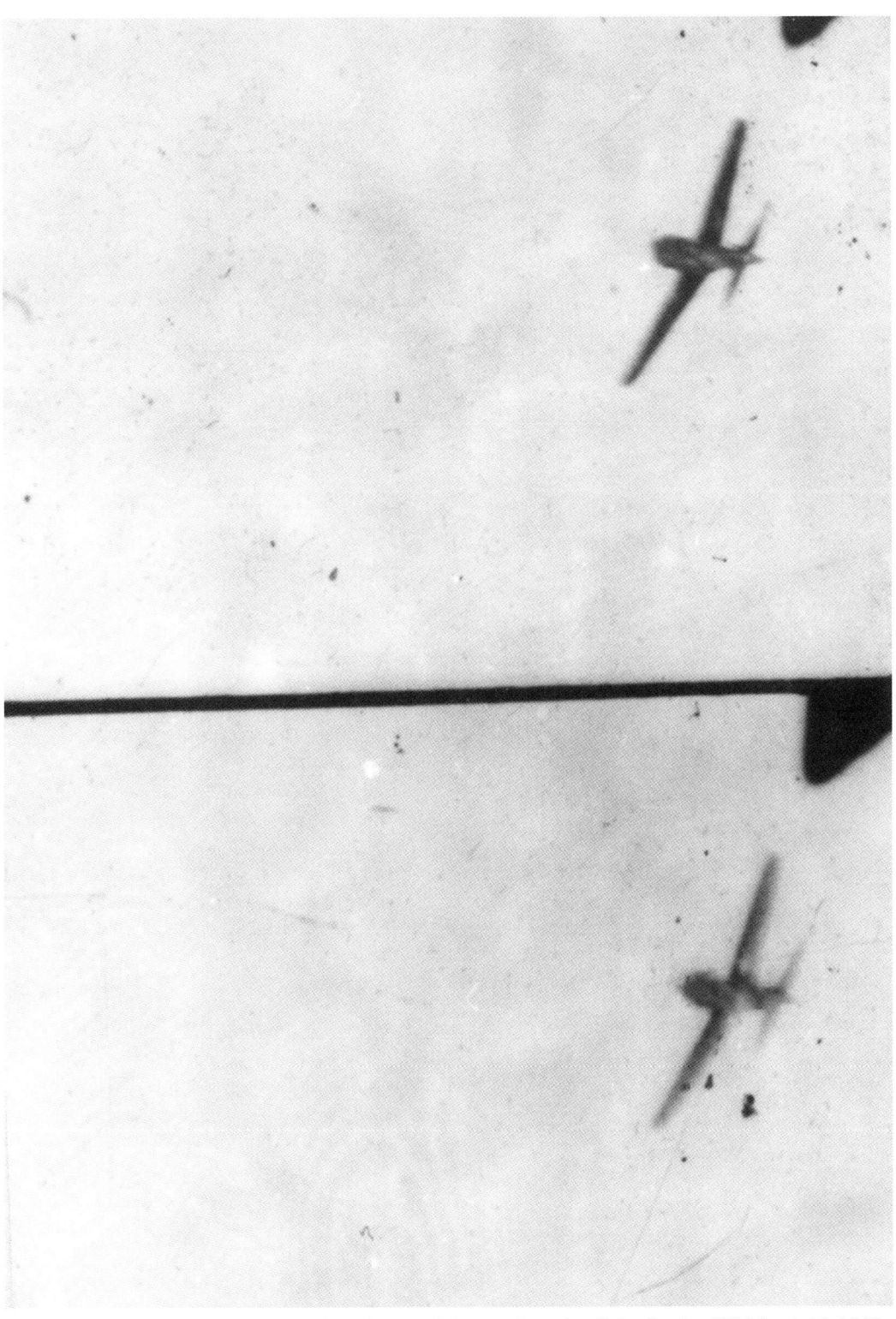

Gun camera image of a Ki-84 "Frank" under attack from a Corsair off the *Bunker Hill*, March 12, 1945, during carrier strikes on Kyushu. (NARA)

Above: Deck crew stand ready in case of fire after an FM-2 Wildcat goes nose down after landing aboard the USS *Shipley Bay* in February 1945. The FM-2 was the ultimate version of the Wildcat to see service during the war. Earmarked for the growing escort carrier force, the FM-2 proved a tough and reliable fighter. By V-J Day, the total Wildcat score of enemy aircraft destroyed stood at 1,514.5 aerial victories. (NARA)

The last dogfight of World War II between U.S. Navy and Japanese fighters occurred on August 15, 1945. Six F6F-5 Hellcats of VF-88 from the carrier *Yorktown* engaged approximately twenty enemy fighters over Atsugi airfield near Tokyo. During the fight, the pilots of VF-88 claimed eight Japanese fighters shot down, but they lost four of their own. Here, Lieutenant Maurice Proctor, one of the two surviving pilots, poses with his crew chief and the single bullet hole in his propeller. (Author's Collection)

U.S. Navy Carriers

The might of the U.S. Navy on full display. Task Force 38, of the U.S. Third Fleet maneuvering off the coast of Japan, August 17, 1945, two days after Japan agreed to surrender. Taken by a USS *Shangri-La* (CV-38) photographer. The aircraft carrier in lower right is the USS *Wasp* (CV-18). Also present in the formation are five other Essex-class carriers, four light carriers, at least three battleships, plus several cruisers and destroyers. (U.S. Naval Historical Center)

Surrender of Japan, September 2, 1945. Navy carrier planes fly in formation over the U.S. and British Pacific Fleet in Tokyo Bay during surrender ceremonies. The USS *Missouri* (BB-63), where the ceremonies took place, is at left. The USS *Detroit* (CL-8) is in the right distance. (U.S. Naval Historical Center)

CHAPTER 2

BRITISH ROYAL NAVY AIRCRAFT CARRIERS

Photographed in a British harbor, circa late 1918, painted in dazzle camouflage, HMS *Argus*. An R-class battleship is in the distance. HMS *Argus* was the first real carrier to enter service with the Royal Navy. Converted from a liner during World War I, it would be used as a training carrier in 1939 and later as an escort carrier. (U.S. Naval Historical Center)

HMS *Furious* at sea with a flight of Blackburn Baffin torpedo planes overhead, 1935–1936. Built as a battle cruiser in World War I, *Furious* was fitted with a flying-off deck. In 1921 it was converted into a fully decked aircraft carrier. Modified in the 1930s, it could carry thirty aircraft. (U.S. Naval Historical Center)

HMS Eagle pictured here in Rio de Janeiro, April 1933. Originally laid down as a battleship in World War I, Eagle was converted into a carrier in 1924. Updated in 1939, it could carry twenty-four aircraft. It would serve in the Indian Ocean and the South Atlantic, but spent most of its time in the Mediterranean protecting convoys to Malta. On August 11, 1942, it was hit by four torpedoes from the German submarine U-73. It sank within eight minutes. (U.S. Naval Historical Center)

HMS *Furious* following reconstruction, 1925. At the beginning of the war *Furious* could carry thirty-six aircraft (Fairey Swordfish and Blackburn Skua). It participated in Allied operations in Norway 1940, convoy escort in the Mediterranean, and Operation Pedestal (the relief convoy for Malta in August 1942). Sent to Norfolk, Virginia, for refit in October 1942, it returned to participate in Operation Torch (the invasion of North Africa) in November. Its last significant contribution was during Operation Tungsten (the FAA strikes against the German battleship *Tirpitz*). (U.S. Naval Historical Center)

HMS *Ark Royal* photographed circa 1939, with one Fairey Swordfish aircraft taking off as another one approaches from astern. When Britain entered the war in September 1939, the Royal Navy had seven carriers, of which the *Ark Royal* was the most modern. Capable of carrying sixty aircraft, it was the most formidable. In its most famous action, Swordfish from *Ark Royal* were responsible for a torpedo hit on the German battleship *Bismarck* on May 26, 1941. This hit caused the *Bismarck*'s rudder to jam, and with no way to maneuver, it was shortly sunk by British battleships. (U.S. Naval Historical Center)

British Royal Navy Aircraft Carriers

HMS *Indomitable* was laid down on November 10, 1937, and commissioned on October 10, 1941. It displaced twenty-three thousand tons with aircraft capacity of 45–55. Armament consisted of eight twin 4.5-inch dual-purpose guns and six eight-barrel 2-pounder pom-poms. Complement was 1,392 men. Armor consisted of flight deck, 3-inch; belt, 4.5-inch; hanger sides, 1.5-inch. (U.S. Naval Historical Center)

HMS *Ark Royal* started the war attached to the Home Fleet at Scapa Flow. On September 22, 1939, three Skuas of 803 Naval Air Squadron (NAS) from *Ark Royal* shot down a Dornier Do-18 flying boat. The *Ark Royal* could carry sixty aircraft and was armed with eight twin 4.5-inch dual-purpose guns and four eight-barrel 2-pounder pom-poms. (U.S. Naval Historical Center)

The clean lines of the HMS *Ark Royal* are evident in this photograph. With a top speed of 31 knots, it was one of the fastest carriers in the world. In this photo, port and starboard radio transmitting masts are raised. During flight operations they would be lowered, flush with the deck. (U.S. Naval Historical Center)

HMS *Audacity* was of the first of many escort carriers built during World War II and the first for the Royal Navy. The need for air cover over convoys to battle the U-boat menace as well as shoot down or chase away Luftwaffe reconnaissance bombers was vital. In its short career, F4F Wildcats (Martlets in Royal Navy service) from *Audacity* shot down five long-range Focke Wulf Fw 200 Condor aircraft. Ironically, it was torpedoed and sunk by a U-boat December 21, 1941. (U.S. Naval Historical Center)

In September 1939 the Royal Navy's air strength was 232 first-line aircraft, more than half of which were Fairey Swordfish. In terms of fighter aircraft, it was equipped with just eighteen two-seat Blackburn Skuas aboard *Ark Royal* and one squadron of Sea Gladiators on HMS *Glorious*. None of these types were particularly effective, with the Skua being both a fighter and a dive-bomber. Powered by a Bristol Perseus engine, it had a top speed of just 225mph. (Author's Collection)

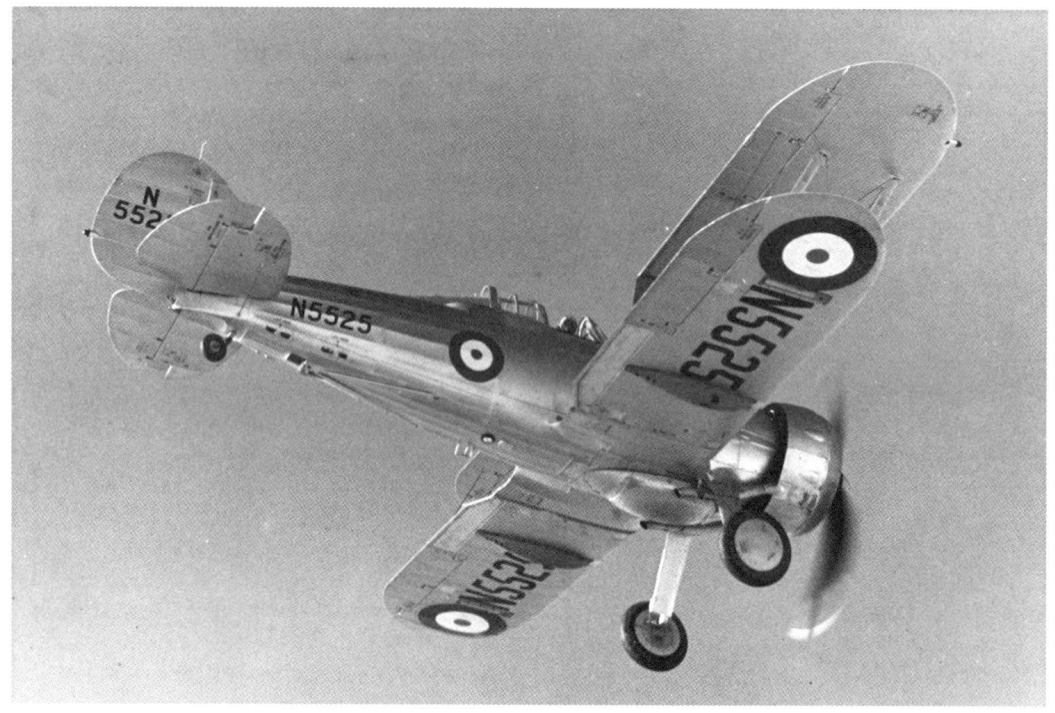

Lacking suitable single-seat fighter aircraft, the Fleet Air was forced to adopt land-based RAF fighters, the first of which was the Gloster Gladiator. These aircraft were navalized with an arrester hook, catapult points, and a fairing for a dinghy. The Mk II version had a top speed of 244mph. Sea Gladiator N5525, pictured here, was one of the twenty-four shipped to Malta and operated by 802 Squadron aboard HMS *Glorious* in the Mediterranean before the outbreak of war. (Matthew Willis)

A Sea Gladiator of 806 NAS crashed on deck aboard HMS *Illustrious* in 1940. This unit operated a few of the Malta-stored Sea Gladiators to supplement its Fulmar fighters and contributed to the defense of Malta when *Illustrious* was severely damaged in January 1941. (Matthew Willis)

The battle against German U-boats continued until the last day of the war. Here a Fairey Swordfish of 816 Squadron warms up for an antisubmarine sweep aboard HMS *Tracker* in early 1945. Each aircraft is armed with eight rocket projectiles. (Author's Collection)

A Fairey Swordfish of 824 NAS takes off from the escort carrier HMS *Striker* during an antisubmarine sweep. This aircraft is armed with the advanced "Fido" torpedo. The air-dropped Fido was a passive acoustic homing torpedo. Once in the water, the torpedo would begin a circular search at a depth of 150ft. Once a U-boat was detected, it would home in and detonate its ninety-two-pound warhead. (Author's Collection)

USS *Saratoga* (CV-3). On January 11, 1942, five hundred miles southwest of Oahu, the *Saratoga* was hit by a single torpedo from the Japanese submarine I-6. It was the first American carrier to be attacked and damaged at the outbreak of war. The *Saratoga* returned to Pearl Harbor for repairs and antiaircraft upgrades. Its 8-inch gun turrets were removed and replaced by four twin 5-inch/.38-cal gun turrets. Her new armament consisted of 16 5-inch/.38-cal guns, nine quadruple 1.1-inch gun mounts, and 32 Oerlikon 20mm cannons. (U.S. Naval Historical Center)

The USS *Wasp* (CV-7) was commissioned in April 1940. The *Wasp*'s unique design was solely driven by the desire to use the remaining 14,700 tons of the Washington Naval Treaty. With less than fifteen thousand tons, it was impossible to build another Yorktown-class carrier, but designers tried to fit as many features as possible of the larger ship into *Wasp*. This resulted in a slightly improved version of *Ranger* but with all its design shortcomings. Seen here in San Diego harbor in June 1942, its flight deck is crowded with thirteen Devastator bombers and twenty F4F-4 Wildcats. (U.S. Naval Historical Center)

The Grumman F4F-3 Wildcat. First flown in 1937, the F4F-3 version was in front-line service with the U.S. Navy in early 1942. The F4F-4 was introduced into the Pacific Fleet in April 1942, replacing the F4F-3. The new fighter featured several important differences including folding wings, six guns (two more than the F4F-3), factory-installed armor, and self-sealing fuel tanks. (Author's Collection)

Grumman F6F-3 Hellcat starting up. This Hellcat is painted in the tricolor camouflage pattern, ordered briefly in spring-summer 1943. Its high performance, heavy firepower, easy handling, and rugged construction made it the standard U.S. carrier fighter from late 1943 until the end of the war. Grumman rolled out the 12,275th and final Hellcat in November 1945. (Author's Collection)

USS *Enterprise* (CV-6), operating in the Pacific, circa late June 1941. It is turning into the wind to recover aircraft. Note its natural wood flight deck stain and dark Measure One camouflage paint scheme. The flight deck was stained blue in July 1941, during camouflage experiments. By June 1942 the *Enterprise*'s antiaircraft defenses had been upgraded. Its .50-cal machine guns had been replaced by thirty-two Oerlikon 20mm cannons. *Enterprise* had an aircraft capacity of eighty-one. (U.S. Naval Historical Center)

The Goodyear built FG-1D Corsair was the F4U-1D version built by Chance Vought. All the F4U-1D/FG-1D models had the R-2800-8W engine with water injection that provided 2,250hp at sea level in the War Emergency Power setting. Top speed was 417mph at nineteen thousand feet with a range of 1,015 miles. (U.S. Naval Historical Center)

Douglas SBD Dauntless and Grumman TBF Avengers ready for takeoff from an escort carrier on training duty, circa mid-1943. The flight deck officer is at left center, while chockmen stand ready to pull chocks on his order. Note yellow training unit markings and red-bordered national insignias on planes. The SBD proved to be the most effective dive-bomber of World War II. In 1942 alone it sank in whole or in part six aircraft carriers, one battleship, three cruisers, four destroyers, one submarine, and fourteen transports (the latter mainly off Guadalcanal). (U.S. Naval Historical Center)

Grumman TBF Avenger comes to a stop after making a qualification landing on a training escort carrier, circa mid-1943. Plane handlers and hook release men are running out from the catwalks. The primary mission of torpedo bombers was sinking enemy carriers and battleships. Range when carrying a torpedo was 1,105nm, top speed was 257mph at twelve thousand feet, and standard cruising speed was 153mph. (U.S. Naval Historical Center)

An F4F Wildcat pilot stores his one-man inflatable life raft pack. All U.S. carrier aircraft were equipped with a one-man life raft and emergency rations. Allied commanders in the Pacific went to great lengths in planning rescue operations to recover pilots who had been forced to ditch. (U.S. Naval Historical Center)

Left: Ditching a damaged or fuel-starved aircraft in the open sea was inherently dangerous. If the aircrew survived the impact and managed to retrieve the one-man life raft, it had water, food, flares, first-aid kit, signaling mirror, and colored dye markers. Unfortunately, many of these items would be lost in the scramble to abandon the sinking aircraft. (U.S. Naval Historical Center)

Below: Arresting gear crewman (in green cap and jersey) operates wheel to raise and lower the flight deck crash barrier on a training escort carrier, circa 1943–1945. If landing aircraft missed catching a wire, they either went around or ran into the crash barrier. (U.S. Naval Historical Center)

USS *Bennington* (CV-20). A USMC ordnance man loads .50-cal machine guns of a F4U-1D Corsair for a strike against the Japanese. The Corsair was armed with six M2 .50-cal machine guns. The inboard and middle guns were provided with 400 rounds; the outboard gun had 375 rounds of ammunition. (U.S. Naval Historical Center)

USS *Bennington* (CV-20). Flight deck crewmen load a modified Mark XIII torpedo into a TBM Avenger torpedo bomber for a strike on Japanese shipping. The Mk XIII proved an extremely unreliable weapon in 1942–1943. By 1944 the Mk XIII was equipped with a plywood "pickle barrel" nose cone drag ring (seen here), which slowed the torpedo mid-drop and absorbed energy on impact. A box-shaped shroud ring on the tail greatly reduced roll, oscillation, and broaches once dropped. (U.S. Naval Historical Center)

USS *Yorktown* (CV-10). Repairing the flight deck. Note fire extinguisher ready to put out any fires caused by welding near the wooden deck. Carriers are essentially floating fuel dumps and munition magazines, and fire was the greatest threat. U.S. flight decks were not armored, but the hangar deck in the Essex class was armored against 1,000-pound bombs. (U.S. Naval Historical Center)

Gunner/radioman and pilot of an SB2C Helldiver go over last-minute flight details. The SB2C was not universally popular with its crews. Power and low-speed handling were particularly deficient. Nevertheless, it sank more Japanese tonnage than any other U.S. aircraft type. (U.S. Naval Historical Center)

USS *Bennington* (CV-20). Grumman F6F-5 Hellcat fighters prepare for takeoff, circa May 1945. These Hellcats are armed with four 3.5-inch Forward Firing Aircraft Rockets (FFAR). (U.S. Naval Historical Center)

Aircraft refueling crew in red caps and jerseys refuel a Grumman TBF-1 on the flight deck of a training escort carrier, mid-1943. Note the ever-present fire extinguisher. Planes were refueled as soon as possible after landing, and the "Smoking Lamp" is out throughout the ship during flight operations. (U.S. Naval Historical Center)

USS *Lexington* (CV-16). Essex-class carriers provided the backbone of the 1943–1945 Fast Carrier Task Force. The Essex-class ships were larger, improved Yorktowns, well-balanced between speed, survivability, and striking power, with a theoretical maximum range of 15,440nm at 15 knots. The Essex class was designed for a crew of 2,386 (215 officers and 2,171 enlisted), but by 1945 complements had swollen to 3,448. (U.S. Naval Historical Center)

USS *Cowpens* (CVL-25). View on the flight deck, probably during working up exercises in summer of 1943. Note the F6F Hellcat, TBF Avenger, and SBD Dauntless aircraft. The Fast Carrier Task Force was augmented by nine 31.5-knot, 11,000-ton Independence-class light carriers. Each could carry 30–40 aircraft. (U.S. Naval Historical Center)

USS *Bunker Hill* (CV-17) burning after being hit by kamikaze suicide planes during the Okinawa operation, May 11, 1945. A Cleveland-class light cruiser is steaming nearby, at left. Fires started by bombs and kamikazes proved deadliest to their crews, and in 1945 several large carriers were severely damaged including the *Bunker Hill* and the USS *Franklin* CV-13, both of which were knocked out of the war. (U.S. Naval Historical Center)

USS *Essex* (CV-9). Landing signal officer (LSO) signals to an incoming plane—"You Are Too High Come Down." The LSO's station was on the port stern, facing backward, so a special windscreen protected him against the thirty-plus knot headwind at his back. (U.S. Naval Historical Center)

USS *Hornet* (CV-12). TBM and SB2C aircraft parked on the after-flight deck, June 12, 1945. USS *Bonne Homme Richard* (CV-31) and two light carriers are in the background. Wartime Carrier Air Group (CAG) size and composition evolved greatly due to changing Japanese tactics and combat experience. By early 1945 an Essex-class carrier carried 103 aircraft: 73 fighters (Hellcats and Corsairs), 15 Helldiver dive-bombers, and 15 Avenger torpedo bombers. (U.S. Naval Historical Center)

The oiler USS *Cahaba* (AO-82) simultaneously refuels USS *Shangri-La* (CV-38) and USS *Iowa* (BB-61), July 8, 1945. Resupply at sea gave the Fast Carrier Task Force the ability to maintain up-tempo operations without having to return to port. This mobility was built on the USN's skill in and emphasis on at-sea replenishment. No other wartime navy so comfortably relied on at-sea refueling, giving the USN a significant operational advantage. (U.S. Naval Historical Center)

USS *Cowpens* (CVL-25). A TBM Avenger landing on board the carrier, at the time of the Marshalls-Gilberts raids, November–December 1943. Note flight deck barrier rigged in the foreground. By 1945 CVLs carried 24–26 F6F Hellcats and 8–9 TBM Avengers. (U.S. Naval Historical Center)

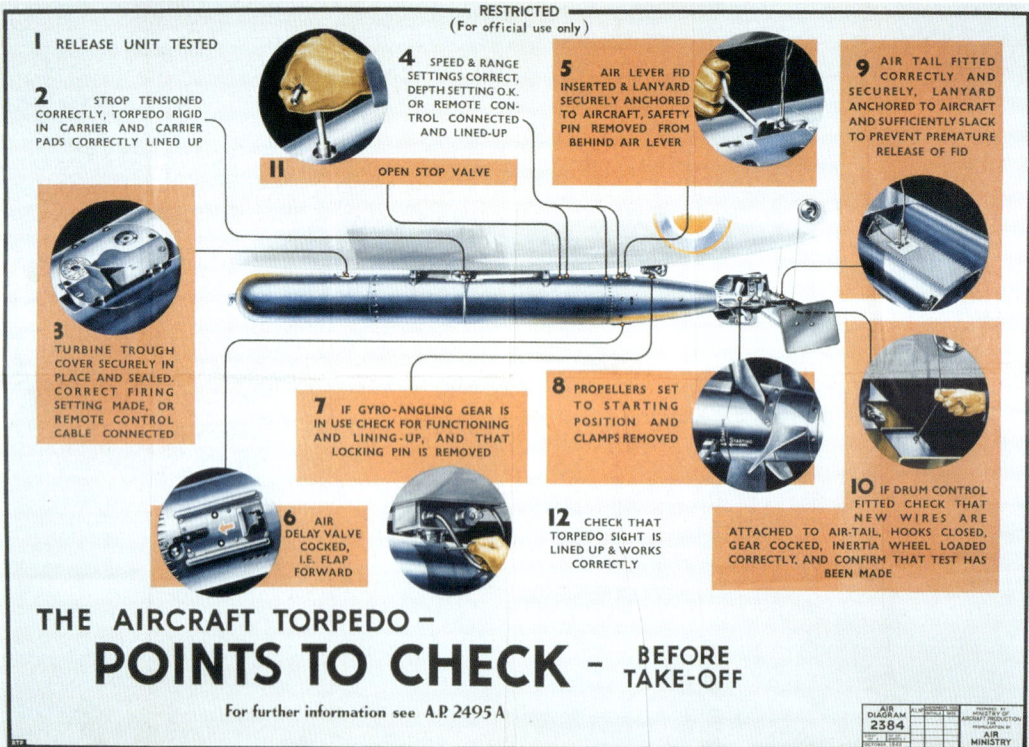

Torpedoes were expensive, complex, and sensitive weapons. Not only did they have to sustain the rough handling on aircraft carrier decks, but they had to withstand a high-speed water entry. This diagram shows the many steps required for the proper installation of an aerial torpedo. During the war the British dropped 609 aircraft torpedoes with 167 hits and 37 probables for a 33.5 percent hit/probable rate. (Author's Collection)

Facing page top: Flight deck officer motions "pull the chocks" with his thumbs as chockmen remove chocks from the wheels of a Grumman F6F-3 Hellcat in preparation for takeoff from a training escort carrier. Note tape on plane's .50-cal gun muzzles. The Hellcat and Corsair were a quantum leap over the existing F4F Wildcat. By 1944 Japanese Zero-sen pilots were overmatched, and in the air-to-air combats that followed they would be decimated. The Hellcats' superb performance was due in part to its Pratt & Whitney's 2,000hp R-2800 Double Wasp eighteen-cylinder radial engine. (U.S. Naval Historical Center)

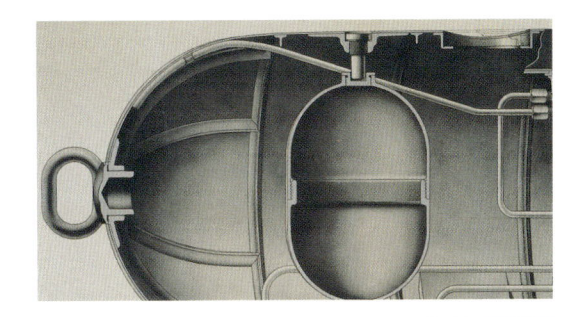

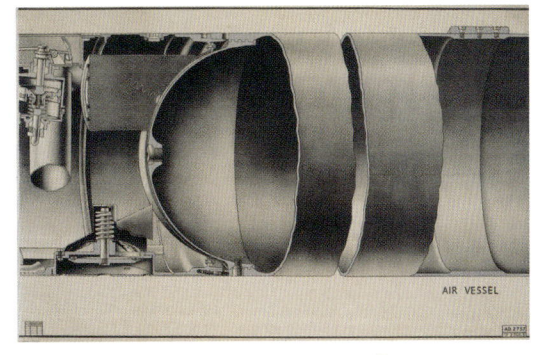

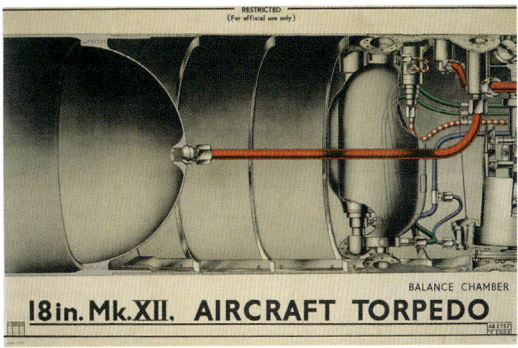

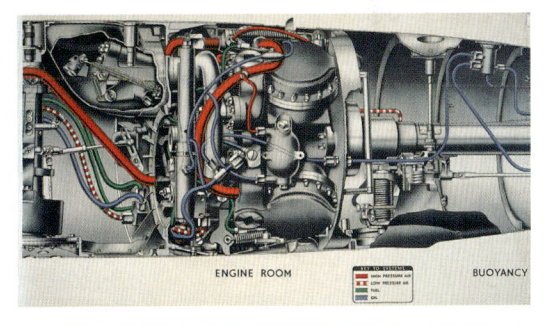

Facing page, bottom, and here: This five-piece air diagram illustration is a depiction of the Mk XII aircraft torpedo. The Mk XII was the standard airborne torpedo for both the RAF and Fleet Air Arm for the first half of the war. It weighed 1,548 pounds with a warhead of 388 pounds. Carriers of all navies carried 2–3 for each torpedo bomber. (Author's Collection)

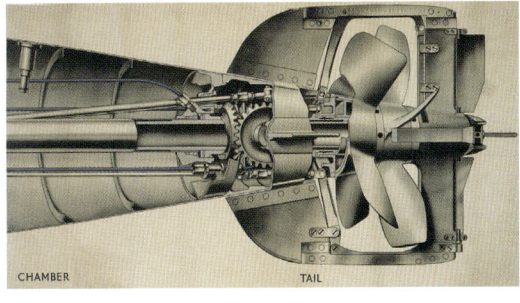

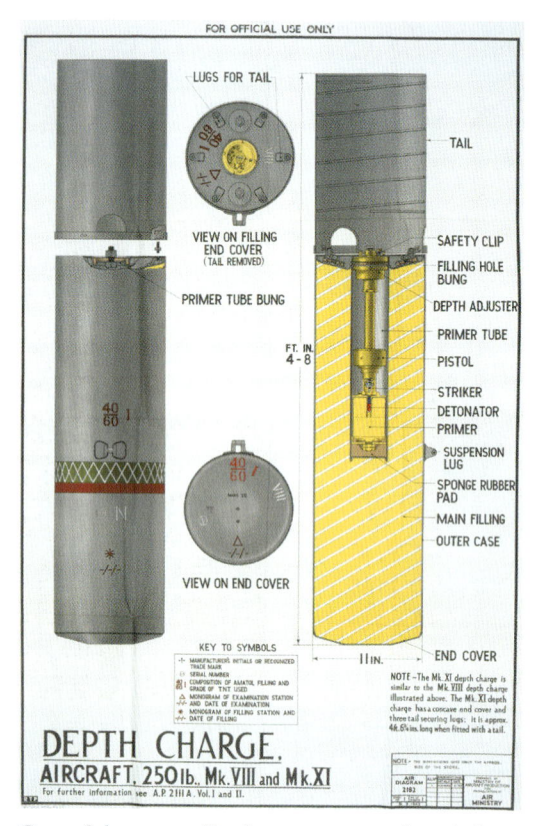

One of the most effective weapons against Axis submarines was the air-dropped depth charge. This cutaway drawing shows the British 250-pound Mk VIII and Mk XI depth charge. The Fairey Swordfish could carry up six 250-pound depth charges. (Author's Collection)

A Fleet Air Arm trainee exits his F4U-1 Corsair after a training flight at Naval Air Station (NAS) Squantum, Massachusetts, in 1943. The best and brightest pilots were selected for fighters, leaving the torpedo and dive-bombers with the rest. (U.S. Naval Historical Center)

An F6F-3 Hellcat aboard HMS *Indomitable*. Here a posed photograph has deck crew in the process of physically moving this aircraft. It would take more than four men to move a Hellcat that weighed 9,328 pounds empty. (Author's Collection)

FAA Martlet MkIIs and Seafires ready for takeoff aboard HMS *Formidable* during Operation Torch. For this operation, *Formidable* carried twenty-four Martlets and six Seafires. (Author's Collection)

Clark Field, the Philippines, 1945. Clark Field was a staging base for the drive toward Japan. This unidentified Seafire III is either a replacement aircraft or one that possibly was used by the Technical Air Intelligence Unit, Southwest Pacific Area located at Clark Field. It would have been used in comparative trials against captured Japanese fighter aircraft. Seafire pilots were credited with thirty-seven aerial victories, fifteen of which were the Mitsubishi Zero-sen. (Author's Collection)

Carrier operations during World War II suffered from high attrition rates. Low on fuel or battle damaged, many aircraft were forced to ditch. This Albacore I—Dinghy Drill training poster outlines the steps required for a successful ditching and deployment of the dinghy. (Author's Collection)

Even with its poor deck handling and landing performance, the Seafire continued in service with the 24 Naval Fighter Wing, seen here during flight operation aboard HMS *Indefatigable* shortly after the war in September 1945. (Author's Collection)

Seafire Mk IIcs aboard HMS *Indomitable* at Scapa Flow, June 1944, shortly after it joined the Eastern Fleet, arriving in the Indian Ocean in July 1944. In February 1945 it joined the British Pacific Fleet. (Author's Collection)

Clear skies and calms seas. Seafire Mk IIIcs of 24 Naval Fighter Wing ready for takeoff shortly after the end of the war, November 1945. In eight days of action between July 17 and August 15, 1945, Seafires of the British Pacific Fleet flew 1,186 sorties over Japan. They were credited with eighty-seven aircraft destroyed on the ground and seven Zero-sens shot down. (Author's Collection)

USS *Yorktown* (CV-10). The view looking aft on the flight deck, November–December 1943, at the time of the Marshalls-Gilberts Operation. In 1943, Essex-class carriers carried a ninety-plane CAG comprising thirty-six Hellcat fighters, thirty-six Dauntless or Helldiver dive-bombers, and eighteen Avenger torpedo bombers. After the carrier turned into the wind, a full deck load strike could be launched in twenty minutes. (U.S. Naval Historical Center)

USS *Yorktown* (CV-10). 20mm Oerlikon cannons firing during target practice in the Pacific, circa summer 1943. Essex-class carriers carried forty-six of these weapons. Equipped with the Mk 14 gyro-stabilized gunsight, seen here, which greatly improved the weapons accuracy. (U.S. Naval Historical Center)

USS *Lexington*. Fighter pilots receive a pre-takeoff briefing in one of the ship's ready rooms. By February 1945, the average U.S. carrier pilot had logged 525 hours' flight time training before his first combat assignment. By comparison, his Imperial Japanese Navy (IJN) counterpart had flown just 275 hours by December 1944, a mere 100 hours by July 1945. (U.S. Naval Historical Center)

Flight deck crew await the return of aircraft to the ship, mid-1943. Farm tractors were adopted as aircraft tugs to ease the burden of deck crews. Essex-class carriers were issued with seven Moto-Tugs. (U.S. Naval Historical Center)

USS *Lexington* (CV-16). A plane director brings an F6F-3 Hellcat fighter down the flight deck after landing. Landing operations, especially after a strike, were fraught with danger. Accidents and crashes were common, making the flight deck one of the most dangerous places to be. (U.S. Naval Historical Center)

USS *Yorktown* (CV-10). Daily calisthenics on the flight deck, during the summer of 1943. During non-flight hours, games of baseball, football, and volleyball could be played on separate portions of the flight deck. Keeping crews active during periods of inactivity was vital for morale and crew efficiency. (U.S. Naval Historical Center)

Grumman F6F-3 Hellcat, aboard USS *Yorktown* (CV-10), gets the takeoff signal from the flight deck officer during shakedown operations in the spring of 1943. Note the man holding the reminder board (says "propeller/flaps") just below the plane's nose. The two forward mounted 40mm quad antiaircraft guns can be seen with the Mk 51-gun director in between. (U.S. Naval Historical Center)

Plane director brings a Grumman F4F Wildcat onto the CVE's catapult. Note the red "Beware of propellers; No smoking" sign on the island of the carrier and red-outlined national insignia on the plane. As planes got heavier and in no-wind conditions, launching by catapult was the only way to get aircraft airborne. It took about ten seconds to launch a plane by deck roll, compared to thirty seconds by catapult. By 1945 fast carriers launched 40 percent of their sorties via catapult. (U.S. Naval Historical Center)

Grumman TBF-1 Avenger receives the takeoff signal. The TBF, though a marked improvement over the obsolete Devastator, was not universally welcomed in the fleet. After the Solomon Islands carrier battle in August 1942, *Enterprise*'s "After Action Report" stated, "The TBF plane, because of its size and weight, is at present a serious potential liability on board aircraft carriers. Too large a number can reduce flight and hangar deck flexibility and slow up flight deck operations at crucial times. A TBF crash on deck can be handled only after long delay and this might well be fatal under certain conditions. It is recommended that the total number of TBF planes in a carrier of the ENTERPRISE type be limited to 12." (U.S. Naval Historical Center)

USS *Santee* (ACV-29). Douglas SBD-3 Dauntless scout bombers and Grumman F4F-4 Wildcat fighters on the ship's flight deck during Operation Torch, the November 1942 invasion of North Africa. Note the yellow Operation Torch markings visible around the fuselage stars of some of these airplanes. Also note the distance and target information temporarily marked on the carrier's flight deck. *Santee* was one of three escort carrier involved in combat during the operation. By the time of the French surrender, the escort carriers had flown 582 sorties for a loss of twenty-nine aircraft. (U.S. Naval Historical Center)

Crewmen from USS *Yorktown* (CV-10) watch as one of their bombers hits a "bull's-eye" on a target sled towed astern of the carrier during bombing practice. Maintaining crew proficiency was one of the keys to Allied victory in the Pacific. (U.S. Naval Historical Center)

A plane director guides a Grumman TBF pilot as he taxies his plane to the catapult track. The USN had long viewed torpedo bombing with suspicion. Torpedoes were expensive, complex, and difficult to deliver, and carried a small warhead. For two years after the Battle of Midway, USN aerial torpedo attacks were virtually suspended against well-defended targets. After modifications to the Mk XIII torpedo, the weapon proved its worth; and in the final year of the war, torpedo bombers would sink Japan's super-battleships *Musashi* and *Yamato*. (U.S. Naval Historical Center)

USS *Lexington* (CV-16) aircraft return to the carrier during the Gilberts operation, November 1943. Crewmen in the foreground are sitting on the wing of an SBD-5 as an F6F-3 lands and a TBF-1 taxies to a parking place on the forward flight deck. In the distance another F6F is seen curving in for its landing approach. During landing operations, aircraft would land every twenty seconds. (U.S. Naval Historical Center)

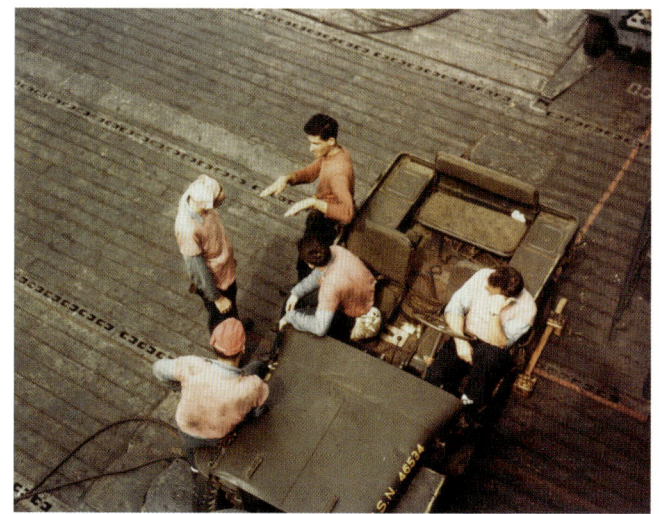

Gasoline crew relaxes around a Jeep flight deck tractor aboard USS *Lexington* during a lull in flight deck operations. Taken during the Gilberts operation, November 1943. Fleets carriers were issued four Jeep flight deck tractors and seven Moto-Tugs; each CVL received two Jeeps and four tractors. (U.S. Naval Historical Center)

USS *Tulagi* (CVE-72). A U.S. Navy F6F "Hellcat" fighter is waved off during a landing attempt after an air-support mission over southern France on Operation Dragoon, D-Day, August 15, 1944. In support of the invasion, the U.S. escort carriers *Tulagi* and *Kasaan Bay* embarked a total of fifty-six F6F Hellcat fighters (including eight night fighters) and five Avengers to provide air cover and ground support for the invasion. (U.S. Naval Historical Center)

5-inch/.38-cal antiaircraft guns firing in gunnery practice, on board an Essex-class aircraft carrier in the Pacific, circa 1944–1945. Note 40mm gun barrels in foreground, also firing, and manned 20mm flight deck gallery beyond. (U.S. Naval Historical Center)

Lwft: A rather happy SBD pilot drinks Dole pineapple juice before taking off on a flight from the USS *Yorktown* (CV-10). He is holding a navigation board and metal compass and is equipped with a late pattern life vest, a .38-cal special revolver, and spare ammunition. (U.S. Naval Historical Center)

Below: From late 1943 onward, the flying deck of virtually all U.S. Pacific fleet carriers was crammed with aircraft. The U.S. Navy's practice of storing aircraft on both the hangar deck and the flight deck (in what was called a deck park) allowed large numbers of fighters, dive-bombers, and torpedo bombers to be embarked. This photo shows the aft deck of the USS *Essex* (CV-9) during its shakedown cruise, March 20, 1943. (U.S. Naval Historical Center)

A TBF-1 Avenger from VT-5 runs up to full power prior to takeoff from the USS *Yorktown* (CV-10), 1944. During the Pacific campaign, the Avenger flew more sorties as a horizontal bomber than in the torpedo bomber role. (U.S. Naval Historical Center)

USS *Intrepid* (CV-11) photographed by Richard Shipman from the rear seat of an SB2C, after taking off to attack the Japanese fleet in the Battle of Sibuyan Sea, October 24, 1944. In the largest air-sea battle up to this point in the Pacific War, U.S. Naval aircraft from Task Force 38 hit the mighty battleship *Musashi* with sixteen bombs and between eleven and fifteen torpedo hits, causing it to sink. (U.S. Naval Historical Center)

Left: USS *Yorktown* (CV-10). Grumman F6F-3 warms up, prior to takeoff, during the ship's shakedown cruise in the spring of 1943. Note chockmen ready to pull chocks from the plane's wheels. This F6F-3 still wears its tricolor paint scheme, which had been authorized for removal the previous February. Deck crews had little time for the constant paint changes that were issued during the war and tended to either ignore them or change what they could in the time permitted. (U.S. Naval Historical Center)

Below: This drawing shows the area of impact and damage caused by a single Japanese kamikaze attack on the USS *Franklin*, October 30, 1944. "6 enemy planes, either 'Zekes' or 'Judys,' 3 of which made suicide runs on *Franklin*. The first plane missed and crashed into the sea about 20 feet from the port side abreast frame 120. At 1426 the second plane struck the flight deck at an angle of approximately 20 degrees with the horizontal somewhat to starboard of the centerline at about frame 127. This plane, with its bomb load intact, crashed through the flight and gallery decks into the hangar." War Damage Report No. 56. (U.S. Naval Historical Center)

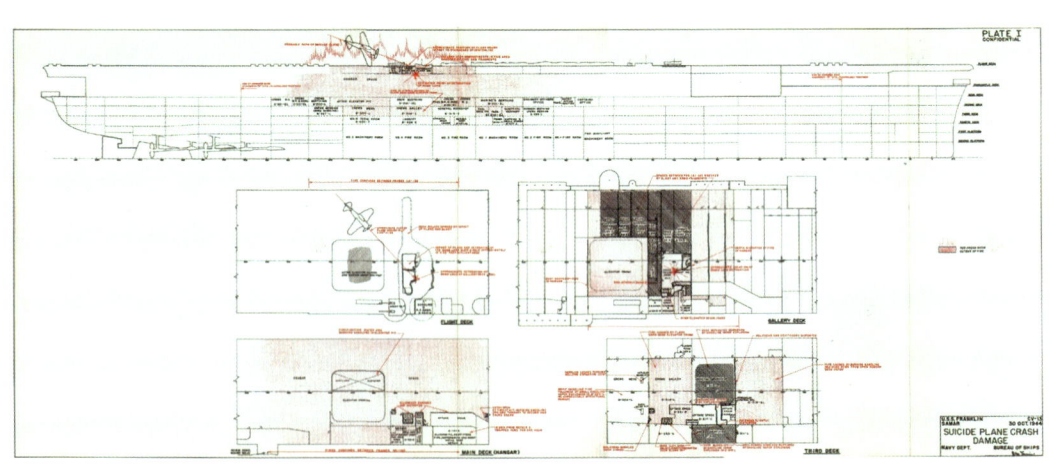

Facing page, bottom: During the carrier battle of the Eastern Solomons August 24, 1942, the USS *Enterprise* suffered three bomb hits and four near misses. This war damage drawing shows the extent of its damage.

"About 1712 on 24 August, *ENTERPRISE* underwent a heavy five-minute attack from more than 30 Japanese dive-bombers during which she received three direct bomb hits and four near-misses. The first bomb struck about two minutes after the start of the attack piercing No. 3 elevator at the flight deck and detonating 42 feet below, between the second and third decks, close to the starboard side.

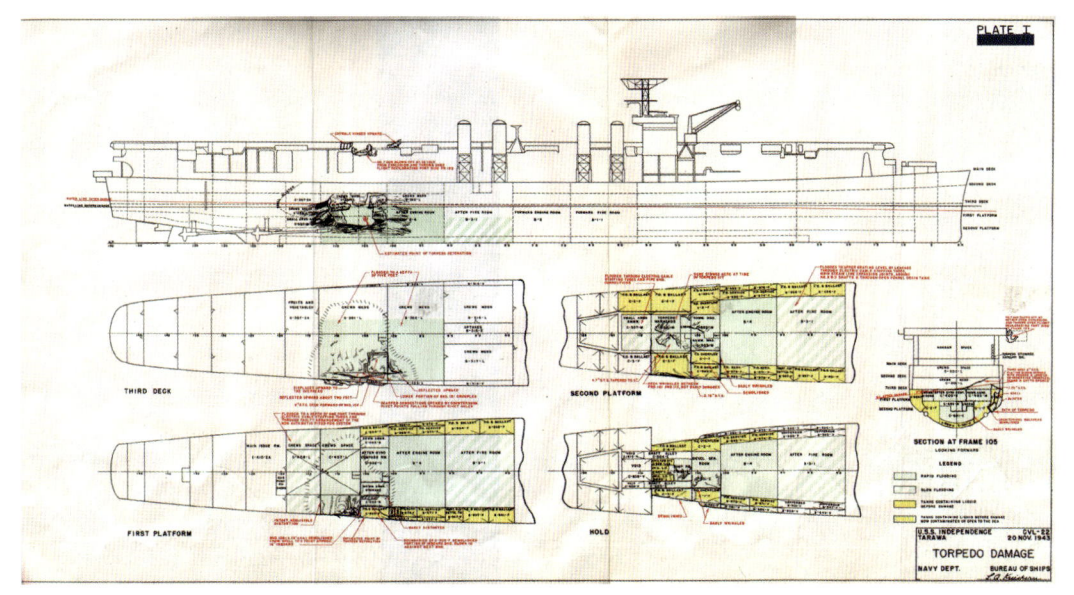

Battle damage diagram USS *Independence*. "On 20 November 1943, USS *Independence* was struck by an aircraft torpedo which detonated upon impact at about frame 105 starboard at the lower edge of the blister. Immediate flooding to the waterline of almost all spaces between bulkheads 91 and 113 a length of 88 feet and including the after engine room, occurred. The ship listed a maximum of 12 degrees to starboard but settled back to 7 degrees within a few moments. (U.S. Naval Historical Center)

"Independence arrived at U.S. Naval Drydocks, Hunters Point on 2 January 1944, and was returned to service with all battle damage repaired and authorized alterations completed on 15 July 1944." War Damage Report No. 52. (U.S. Naval Historical Center)

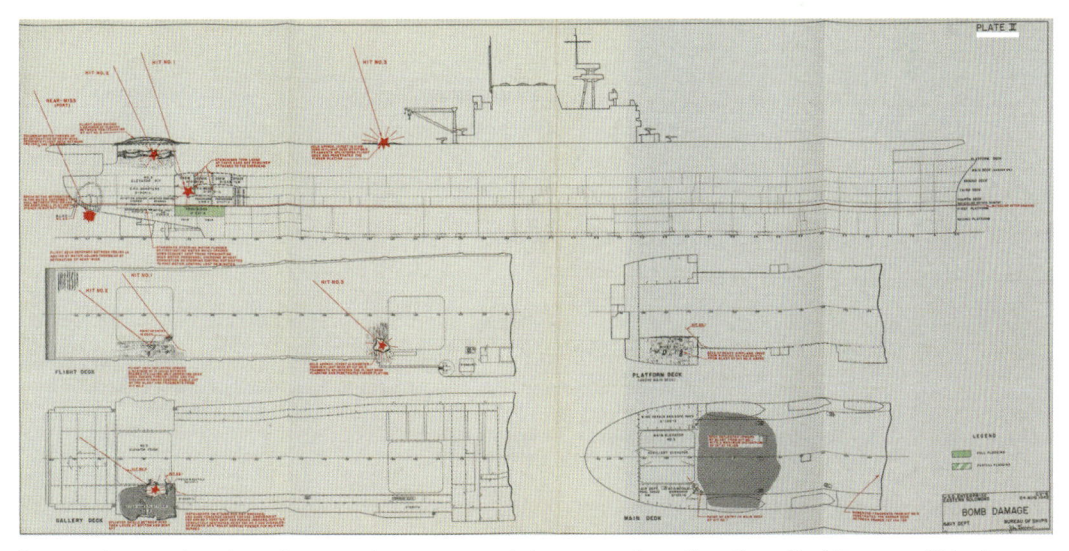

It caused extensive, though not serious structural damage, minor flooding, disablement of No. 3 elevator and several stubborn fires. Despite the damage, ENTERPRISE commenced landing planes within an hour after the engagement. The following day, however, she proceeded to Pearl Harbor for repairs." War Damage Report No. 59. (U.S. Naval Historical Center)

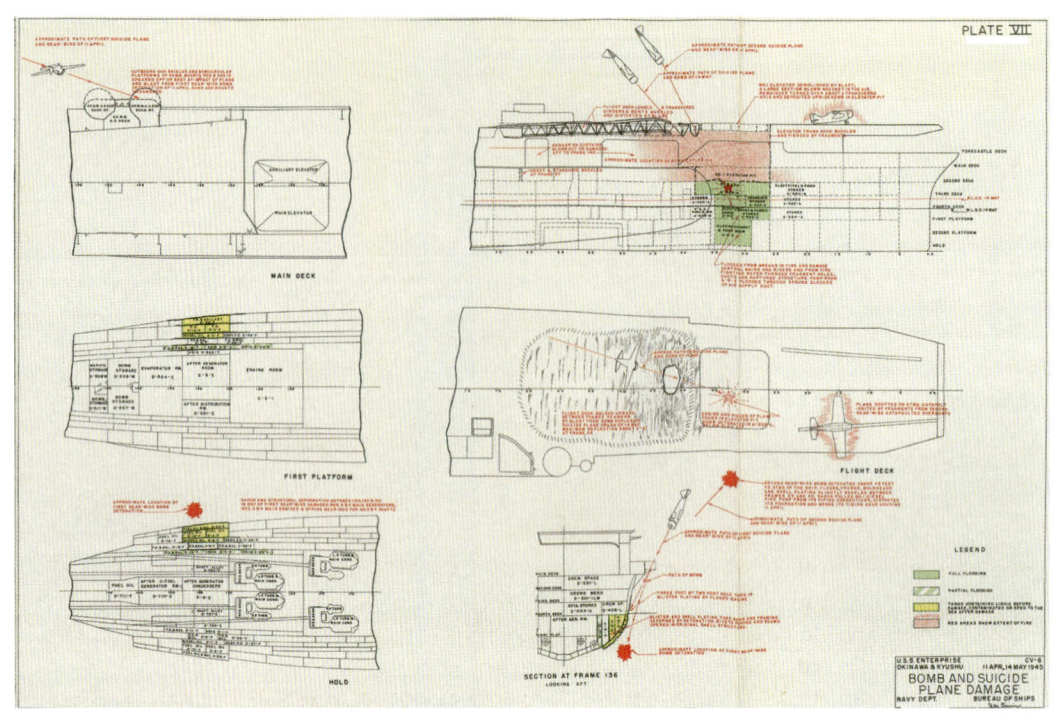

Battle damage diagram shows the hits the USS *Enterprise* sustained by two separate kamikaze attacks on April 11 and May 14, 1945. "During the period of the war she was damaged by the enemy on six separate occasions by 13 hits or near-misses from bombs or suicide planes. In addition, she was damaged by a fire caused by the detonation of a 'friendly' 5-inch anti-aircraft shell. In all cases but one, her excellent damage control organization prevented serious consequences and enabled *ENTERPRISE* to continue in action. Damage to her flight deck which resulted from the suicide plane crash of 14 May 1945 so impaired her operating efficiency that she was forced to retire the following day." War Damage Report No. 59. (U.S. Naval Historical Center)

Facing page bottom: Battle damage diagram shows the torpedo damage that the USS *Liscome Bay* suffered and the escape routes that the remaining crew took after a torpedo hit from a Japanese submarine and the subsequent internal explosion. "*LISCOME BAY* sank some 23 minutes after being torpedoed. Approximately three-fourths of her complement were lost with her. Results of this explosion were disastrous. The ship's structure aft of the forward bulkhead of the aft engine room was generally demolished and there were no survivors aft of this point. The hangar deck was destroyed aft of frame 110 and the flight deck was missing aft of frame 101." War Damage Report No. 45. (U.S. Naval Historical Center)

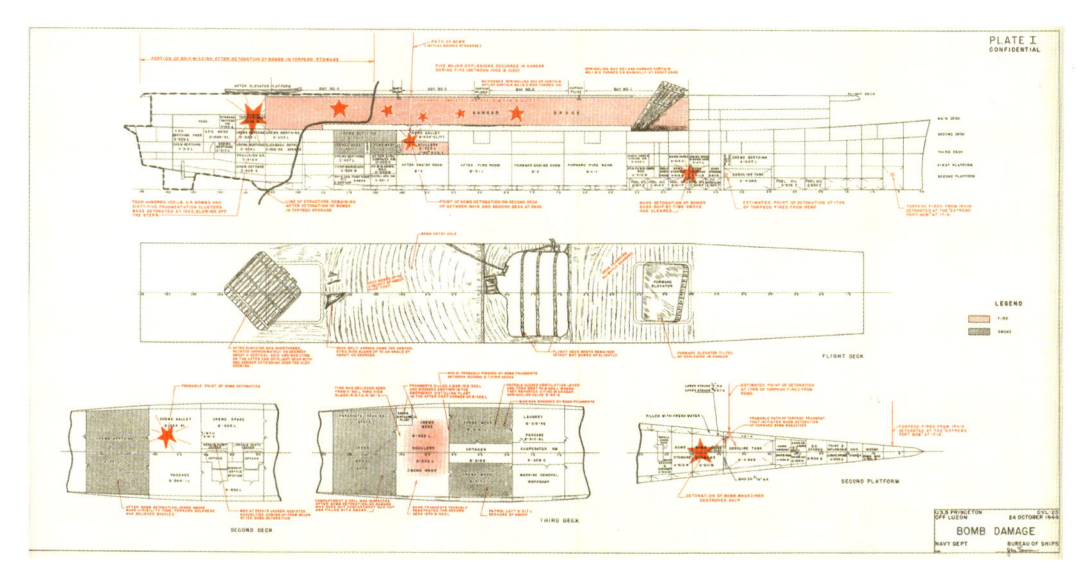

The carrier *Princeton* (CVL-23) was hit by an estimated 250kg GP bomb on the morning of October 24, 1944, while participating in the Battle of Leyte Gulf off the coast of Luzon about 150 miles east of Manila. "At 0938 a single Japanese bombing plane Type JUDY dived out of a low cloud cover ahead of PRINCETON and scored a bomb hit about 15 feet to port of the centerline at frame 98 on the flight deck. The bomb passed through the flight deck, leaving a hole between 14 and 16 inches in diameter, went through a torpedo plane on the hangar deck, pierced the hangar and main decks and detonated in B-204-2L on the second deck or just above that deck." War Damage Report No. 62. Fire quickly spread throughout the hanger deck, causing several large internal explosions that doomed the ship. Shortly, it was sent to the bottom by torpedoes from destroyers *Irwin* and *Reno*. (U.S. Naval Historical Center)

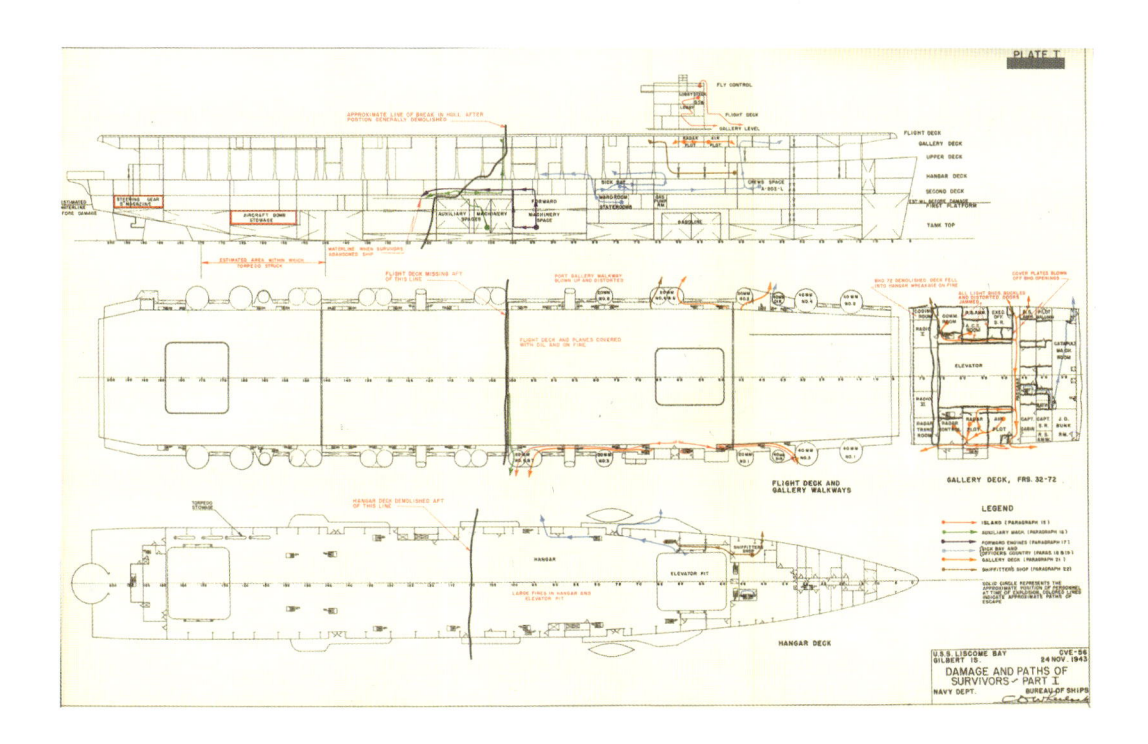

The skipper of Carrier Air Group 15 aboard the USS *Essex* (CV-9), Cdr. David McCampbell, is photographed in his F6F-3 Hellcat "Minsi III" adorned with twenty-one Japanese kill flags. McCampbell would be the U.S. Navy's leading ace of the war, credited with thirty-four confirmed aerial victories; these included seven in one day on June 19, 1944, and nine on October 24. The Hellcat and its pilots proved superior to the much-vaunted Zero-sen. From October 5, 1943, until the end of 1944, U.S. Navy Hellcat pilots claimed approximately 1,540 A6M Zero-sen fighters shot down. During that same period, the U.S. Navy lost 167 carrier-based and 23 land-based Hellcats in aerial combat, between Zero-sens, Japanese bombers, and other Japanese fighter types. Hellcats ultimately produced 305 USN/USMC aces and claimed 5,163 kills against 270 total air-to-air losses, including a 13:1 kill ratio against the Zero. (Author's Collection)

Wherever the U.S. Fast Carrier Task Force went, Zero-sens were destroyed in large numbers. This wrecked A6M5 on Kwajalein Atoll in February 1944 stands in testament to the crushing power of the U.S. and British Pacific Fleets. (Author's Collection)

British Royal Navy Aircraft Carriers 69

Skua serial number L2870 after a deck-landing accident aboard HMS *Courageous* in 1939. This aircraft was used for deck-landing trials. (Matthew Willis)

Skuas of 800 and 803 NAS ranged aboard HMS *Ark Royal* June 12, 1940, shortly before the disastrous raid on the German battleship *Scharnhorst* that lay in Trondheim harbor, Norway. Shortly after midnight on June 13, fifteen Skuas took off. Even before they could begin their dives, the Skuas were intercepted by Luftwaffe Bf 109s and Me 110s. Just seven Skuas made it back to the carrier, and no hits were recorded on the *Scharnhorst*. (Matthew Willis)

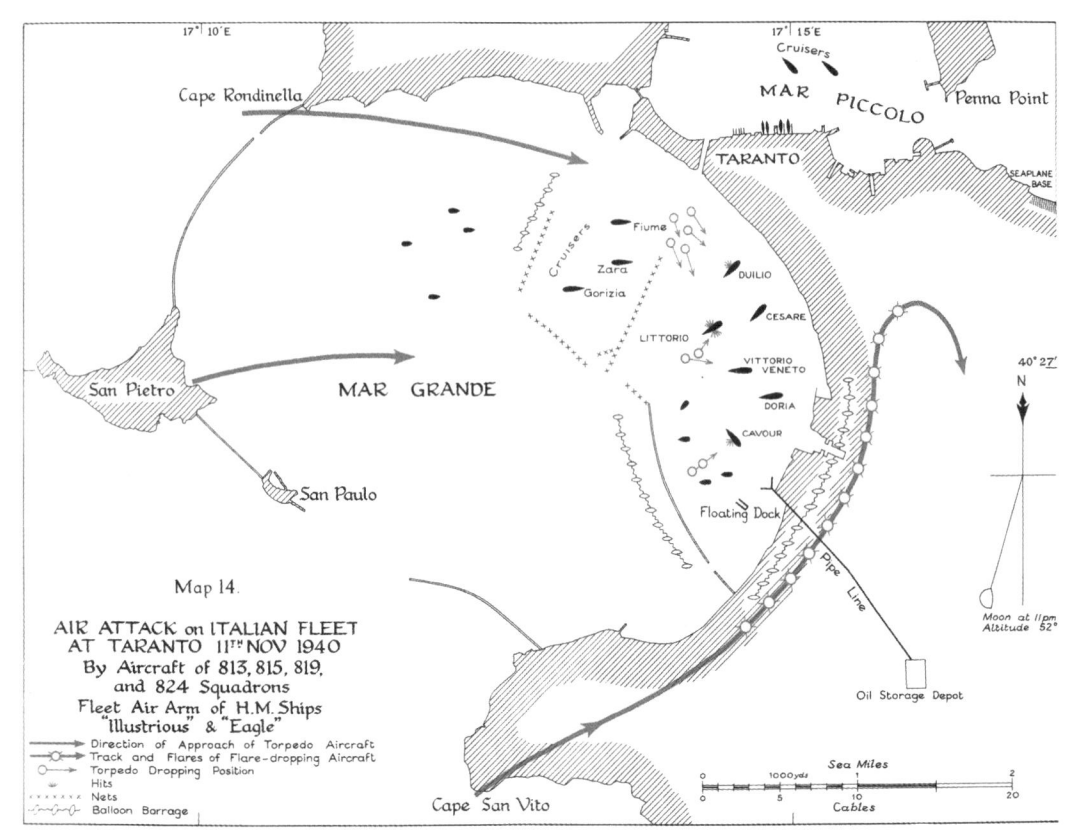

Operation Judgement was one of the greatest carrier attacks of World War II. On the evening of November 10, twenty-one Swordfish lifted off from HMS *Illustrious* in two waves. Their target was Taranto Harbor and the six Italian battleships anchored. In the first wave, six Swordfish were armed with torpedoes, four with bombs, and two with a mixture of bombs and flares. The flare droppers led the way, dropping their flares on the eastern side of the harbor to illuminate the battleships for the torpedo bombers. The second wave consisted of five torpedo bombers, two flare droppers, and the remaining two armed with bombs. The Italian battleship *Littorio* was hit by three torpedoes, the *Caio Duilio* by one, and the *Contvi di Cavour* by one. Just two Swordfish were shot down during the raid. (Author's Collection)

HMS *Victorious* in preparation for antishipping raids in Norwegian waters, October 1941. Here a Fairey Albacore prepares to land with two Fairey Fulmars on the forward deck in front of the crash barrier. *Victorious* was the second of the Illustrious-class carriers and could carry thirty-six aircraft. (Author's Collection)

HMS *Furious* preparing to launch two Seafires for northern convoy protection patrols in July 1943. The U.S. battleship *South Dakota* (BB-57) is following closely astern. (Author's Collection)

HMS *Formidable* with Seafires of 885 NAS Squadron on outriggers during Operation Torch, the invasion of North Africa by American and British troops November 8, 1942. This would be the Seafires' baptism of fire. Seafires claimed five enemy aircraft shot down for the loss of twenty-one aircraft due to operational causes. (Matthew Willis)

HMS *Indomitable* striking an Fairey Albacore aircraft below. The Fairey Albacore was designed to replace the Fairey Swordfish. Whereas its enclosed cockpit offered more protection and comfort for its crew, its performance was comparable, and it never did replace the Swordfish completely. By 1943 Albacore squadrons began receiving the new Blackburn Barracuda torpedo/dive-bomber. (U.S. Naval Historical Center)

HMS *Victorious* operating a small flight of six Seafire IIBs for air defense during operation Torch. Astern are the escort carriers HMS *Biter* and *Avenger*, with Sea Hurricanes ranged on deck. For the landings, the Royal Navy deployed three fleet carriers and four escort carriers. (Matthew Willis)

Seafire IIcs ranged forward on HMS *Indomitable* during Operation Husky, the invasion of Sicily July 9, 1943. In the background are the battleship HMS *Rodney* and a destroyer. With its large forward lift, *Indomitable* could carry more of the early non-folding version of the Seafire and operated three squadrons, 807, 819, and 880 NAS. But its deployment was cut short after being torpedoed by a lone Luftwaffe Ju 88. (Matthew Willis)

Deck-landing accident on HMS *Attacker* during the Salerno landings, the invasion of Italy on September 9, 1943. This unidentified Seafire (879 or 886 NAS) missed the wires and hit the barrier, tearing off its Merlin engine. This operation would cement the Seafire's reputation as a dismal carrier fighter. Operating from five escort carriers and two fleet carriers, 106 Seafires were available. *Most of the Seafire pilots had very little experience in their new machines.* This led to numerous deck accidents. In total, some seventy Seafires would be lost or rendered inoperable through accidents during these four days of intensive and difficult low-wind operations. But they did their job and protected the fleet from aerial attack. (Matthew Willis)

Facing page bottom: British carrier pilots had to endure some of the harshest flying conditions during the war. Here an F4F Martlet (Wildcat) is covered in snow aboard the escort carrier HMS *Activity* during an Artic convoy patrol. In the background is a Fairey Swordfish armed with eight air-to-ground rockets and an outboard rack of flares. (Matthew Willis)

British Royal Navy Aircraft Carriers 75

Operation Bowery. The U.S. carrier *Wasp* (CV-7) and HMS *Eagle* (in the background) launched sixty-four Spitfire Mk VCs on May 9, 1942, to reinforce the fighters on Malta. Here deckhands add weight to the tail as Spitfire BR344 is run up prior to launch. A Grumman F4F Wildcat of VF-71 is parked to the left. (Author's Collection)

Escort carriers played a pivotal role during World War II. These small carriers provided convoy escort, at the same time performing other useful roles such as hunting U-boats, transporting aircraft, providing air and ground attack support for amphibious landings, and refueling other escort vessels at sea. Here HMS *Striker* prepares three Fairey Swordfish for launch with two F4F Martlets (Wildcats) off to the side. *Striker* could carry twenty aircraft. (Author's Collection)

Operations in the Atlantic, February 1944. A Sea Hurricane Mk IIc of 824 NAS is parked at the aft end of HMS *Striker*. The Mk IIc was the most heavily armed single-seat fighter to see service with the Fleet Air Arm (FAA). Armament consisted of four 20mm Hispano cannons with one hundred rounds per gun. Eventually some eighteen FAA squadrons would operate Sea Hurricanes during the war. (NARA)

HMS *Campania* was a British-built escort carrier converted from a refrigerated cargo ship hull. Capable of carrying twenty aircraft, it had a top speed of 18 knots and a range of thirteen thousand miles at 16 knots. Photographed on June 22, 1944, seven Fairey Swordfish torpedo bombers and probably two Grumman Martlet fighters are visible on flight deck. (U.S. Naval Historical Center)

Fairey Albacore flying over HMS *Indomitable* in the Indian Ocean, 1942. Four Hawker Sea Hurricane Mk IBs can be seen on deck, three on outriggers. *Indomitable* joined the Eastern Fleet, arriving in the Indian Ocean in December 1941, there until July 1942. It rejoined the Eastern Fleet in July 1944 and operated against Japanese targets in the East Indies until February 1945, when it became part of the British Pacific Fleet. (Matthew Willis)

A Fairey Fulmar on deck testing its guns while on distant cover for a convoy. A King George V-class battleship turns to port in the background. The empty cartridge cases can be seen falling from the ejector chutes beneath the wing. As the Fleet Air Arm's first long-range fleet fighter, the Fulmar was always a stop-gap measure and one of the forgotten fighters of World War II. The important role this fighter played in the development of carrier air-group tactics and roles was immense. Its achievements in protecting fleets and convoys operating in the various "bomb alleys" of the Mediterranean should not be overlooked. (Matthew Willis)

Fulmars from 800 and 809 NAS wait to take off from HMS *Victorious*. The Fulmar was armed with eight .303-inch machine guns with 750 rounds per gun. This compared to the 334 rounds per gun carried in the Sea Hurricane. (Matthew Willis)

A Fulmar is airborne after a catapult launch off from the escort carrier HMS *Pretoria Castle*. Although it occasionally operated in support of convoys, *Pretoria Castle* spent most of its career as a training ship for Fleet Air Arm aircrew. (Matthew Willis)

Fulmars of 806 Squadron NAS and Wildcats aboard HMS *Illustrious* in the Indian Ocean, December 1942. The battleship HMS *Valiant* fires the main guns during a practice shoot. In the final accounting, the Fulmar proved a worthy fighter, credited with 122 kills, the highest total of all the fighters employed by the FAA. FAA fighters would tally 455 aerial victories during the war. Just forty Fulmars were lost to enemy action. The last Fulmar fighter squadron was withdrawn in March 1943. (Matthew Willis)

Hawker Sea Hurricanes of 885 NAS HMS *Victorious*, August 1942, prior to Operation Pedestal. In August 1942 the besieged British island of Malta was in desperate need of supply. Thirteen large, fast merchant ships and a tanker were assembled with protection provided by three carriers, *Indomitable*, *Victorious*, and *Eagle* with seventy-two fighters on board (a mix of Fulmars, Wildcats, and Sea Hurricanes). On August 11 German and Italian aircraft began their attacks. The battle, both in the air and on the sea, would last seven days. In the end the British would lose HMS *Eagle* (sunk by a U-boat), nine merchant ships, two cruisers, and a destroyer. Thirty-two thousand short tons of supplies were delivered, giving the island forces ten more weeks of supply. (Matthew Willis)

The Sea Hurricane, like the Seafire that was to follow, was a product of desperation. Despite its shortcomings it was a welcome addition to the fleet, and for a year it would be the fastest fighter in the FAA's inventory. Sea Hurricanes carried only enough fuel to sustain themselves for one hour at combat power and 4.5 hours at full-economical settings. The Fulmar and Martlet could stay aloft for 2 hours, 2 3/4 hours under combat power, and 6 hours economical. The consequence of this was carriers being forced to turn into the wind far more often to take off and land Sea Hurricanes. Hawker Sea Hurricanes of 885 NAS HMS *Victorious*, August 1942, during Operation Pedestal. (Matthew Willis)

Sea Hurricane Mk IICs of 825 NAS with outer cannons removed aboard HMS *Vindex*. *Vindex* was a Nairana-class escort carrier, converted from cargo ship hulls. The three Nairana-class escort carriers performed well in the extreme conditions found in the North Atlantic and Arctic, so ultimately all three of them saw service protecting the Arctic convoys. *Vindex* carried twenty aircraft and fifty-two thousand gallons of aviation fuel. (Matthew Willis)

HMS *Victorious* at Noumea in 1943. After the carrier battle of Santa Cruz in October 1942, the U.S. Navy has just one operational carrier in service, the USS *Saratoga*. It was at this critical junction the U.S. Navy asked Britain for help. In December 1942, *Victorious* arrived at the Norfolk Navy Yard for modifications. On February 3, 1943, it left Norfolk and headed to the Pacific with fifty-two aircraft: thirty-six Martlet IVs in 882, 896, and 898 Squadrons, as well as sixteen freshly delivered TBF Avengers of 832 Squadron. On May 17, 1943, *Victorious* joined the USS *Saratoga* off Noumea in the New Hebrides to become the only two operational Allied carriers in the Pacific. By the end of July, the first of the U.S. Navy's new Essex- and Independence-class carriers were reaching operational status in the Central Pacific. Having seen no enemy action during its cruise, HMS *Victorious* returned to the Atlantic theater of operations. (Author's Collection)

Swordfish ASW aircraft from 811 NAS takes off from the escort carrier HMS *Biter*. In a report written by the commanding officer of Air Station Crail in 1943 on the state of torpedo training for Swordfish pilots, his comments on the Swordfish were quite accurate: "The Swordfish was, it is true, designed as a torpedo bomber, but it is its unique qualities as a convoy escort plane which have kept it on the production line, and it is a such that it should be thought of. As a torpedo bomber for use in daylight against anything but undefended merchant ships, its day is done." (NARA)

HMS *Formidable* in the Indian Ocean, 1944. On deck are five Seafires and seven Wildcats. Maximum speed: 30½ knots. Fuel capacity: 4,840 tons. Armor—flight deck: 3-inch; belt and hangar sides: 4.5-inch. Armament: eight twin 4.5-inch dual-purpose guns, six eight-barrel 2-pounder pom-poms. Aircraft capacity: thirty-six aircraft. Complement: 1,229 men. (Author's Collection)

HMS *Implacable*. The *Implacable* entered service with the Home Fleet in June 1944. With its complement of sixty aircraft, it flew strikes against German shipping and harbors until March 1945. In April 1945 it joined the British Pacific Fleet (BPF) and two months later began strikes against the Japanese base at Truk Lagoon. In July, it began launching strikes against Japanese shipping and bases in Japanese home waters. (U.S. Naval Historical Center)

British Royal Navy Aircraft Carriers

A Barracuda Mk II is launched from the aircraft carrier HMS *Glory* during the carrier's workup period, with the aid of the hydraulic "accelerator" or catapult. Entering service in early 1943, as a replacement for the Swordfish and Albacore, the Barracuda was a dual-purpose torpedo and dive-bomber. Although it was reasonably effective, its crews regarded it as dangerous and difficult to fly. (Matthew Willis)

Barracudas of 827 NAS prepare for takeoff aboard HMS *Victorious* during Operation Tungsten, strikes against the German battleship *Tirpitz*, April 3, 1944. These aircraft are armed with the 1,600-pound AP bomb, the heaviest piece of ordnance carried in these strikes. Thirty-two Barracudas in two waves would participate. Barracuda pilots managed to hit the *Tirpitz* with three 1,600-pound AP bombs, and a mix of nine 500-pound SAP and MC bombs and one 600-pound AS (MC) bomb. The damage was reported as extensive, but later photo reconnaissance revealed that it was largely superficial. (Matthew Willis)

A battle-damaged Barracuda strikes the crash barrier upon landing aboard HMS *Victorious*. This aircraft was one of the thirty-two Barracudas involved in the strikes against the German battleship *Tirpitz* during Operation Tungsten. One Barracuda was shot down by flak during the raid. (Matthew Willis)

The German cargo ship *Deutsche Levante* under attack by Seafires of 801 NAS and Avengers from 846 and 852 NAS in Aaramsund, Norway, September 12, 1944. (Matthew Willis)

A Wildcat from 881 NAS crashes through the crash barrier and lands upside-down on board HMS *Fencer*. The Wildcat proved a versatile and reliable fighter serving from the Arctic Circle to the heat of the Indian and Pacific Oceans. FAA Martlet/Wildcats were credited with sixty-seven aerial victories during the war. (NARA)

Operation Judgement, May 4, 1945, was an attack on the U-boat base at Kilbotn, near Harstad, Norway. This proved to be the last offensive operation by the Home Fleet as the war in Europe came to a close. Three escort carriers were involved, HMS *Searcher*, HMS *Trumpeter*, and HMS *Queen*. Twenty-four Wildcats (eight armed with 250-pound bombs) and sixteen Avengers with four 500-pound bombs participated in the attack. (Author's Collection)

HMS *Indefatigable* heads through the Suez Canal on its way to the Pacific in late 1944. The Seafires of 894 NAS are still wearing their standard National markings. Prior to moving to the Pacific, the *Indefatigable* was involved in Operation Mascot, an attack on the German battleship *Tirpitz*. Seafire Squadrons 887 and 984 NAS provided CAPs and fighter sweeps. (ww2images.com)

A Grumman Avenger of 845 NAS during a catapult launch, while in the harbor, from the escort carrier HMS *Empress*, near Trincomalee, Ceylon, early 1945. Catapult launches were used when the wind was light or nonexistent. Catapult launches took longer when compared to the preferred method of turning into the wind and using the speed of the carrier to provide for a short takeoff. (Author's Collection)

Fleet Air Arm Avenger "4H-Q" of 854 NAS ends up on its nose after missing the wires, early January 1945. No. 854 NAS aboard the *HMS Illustrious* along with 820, 849, and 857 aboard HMS *Illustrious*, HMS *Victorious*, and HMS *Indomitable* formed the Avenger strike force assigned to the two-phase attack on Sumatran oil fields starting on January 24. (Author's Collection)

No. 854 NAS Avengers outbound on the second Sumatran strike that took place on January 29, 1945. The strike group was nearly identical to that of the first raid on the January 24 with Lt. Cdr. W. J. Mainprice, CO of *Illustrious*'s 854 Squadron leading the way. (Author's Collection)

Smoke from the second Sumatran oil field strike confirms another success on January 29, 1945. As the Fleet Air Arm Avengers head for the rendezvous point after the attack, two Japanese Ki-44s can be seen in the upper left, diving into the attack. When the raid was over, six Avengers ditched near the fleet. These crews were rescued, but unfortunately eleven other Avengers were shot down or forced to land. Avenger crews claimed two Ki-44 "Tojos" shot down. (Frank Mitchell via Howard J. Mitchell)

Avenger Mk II JX383 of 849 NAS based on the aircraft HMS *Victorious* crosses the Sumatran coast after the second strike on the Japanese oil fields on January 24, 1945. (Author's Collection)

When the British Pacific Fleet began operations, it was equipped with thirty-eight Grumman Hellcats with 1839 and 1844 NAS aboard HMS *Indomitable*. Missing the wires, Hellcat 5A/JX758 of 1839 NAS goes over the side of the *Indomitable* on February 27, 1945. (Andrew Thomas)

A Firefly Mk 1 of 1770 NAS unfolds its wings in preparation for the Sumatra oil refinery raid on January 24, 1945. During this mission, the Firefly scored its first air-to-air kill. The victim was a Ki-43 "Oscar." (Andrew Thomas)

Corsair IIs and Barracuda Mk IIs crowd the front deck of HMS *Illustrious*, January 24, 1945. Corsair 7R/JT433, flown by Lt. Percy Cole of 1833 NAS, was credited with a Ki-45 "Nick" shot down on that day. (Via Andrew Thomas)

A Firefly from 1771 NAS from HMS *Implacable* heads for a target in Japan, July 1945. At this stage of the war, rocket-armed Fireflies were flying "Ramrod" missions—offensive fighter sweeps over Japan. The Firefly had ample armament with four 20mm electro-pneumatic Hispano cannon. The inner cannons were fed with 175-round belts, with 145 for each of the outer guns. (Andrew Thomas)

Avenger overboard. During operations against Sakishima in 1945, this Avenger suffered engine failure shortly after taking off from HMS *Smiter*. The crew can be seen scrambling into the water. (Author's Collection)

HMS *Victorious* Corsairs and Avengers flew strikes against the Japanese homeland until August 11, 1945. With its aircrew exhausted and supplies running low, it was ordered out of the line to return to Sydney. Here the crew hear the announcement of V-J Day. During its Pacific operations, *Victorious*'s air group consisted of 849 Squadron (fourteen Avengers), 1834, 1836 Squadrons (thirty-seven Corsairs), 2 Walrus ASR. (Author's Collection)

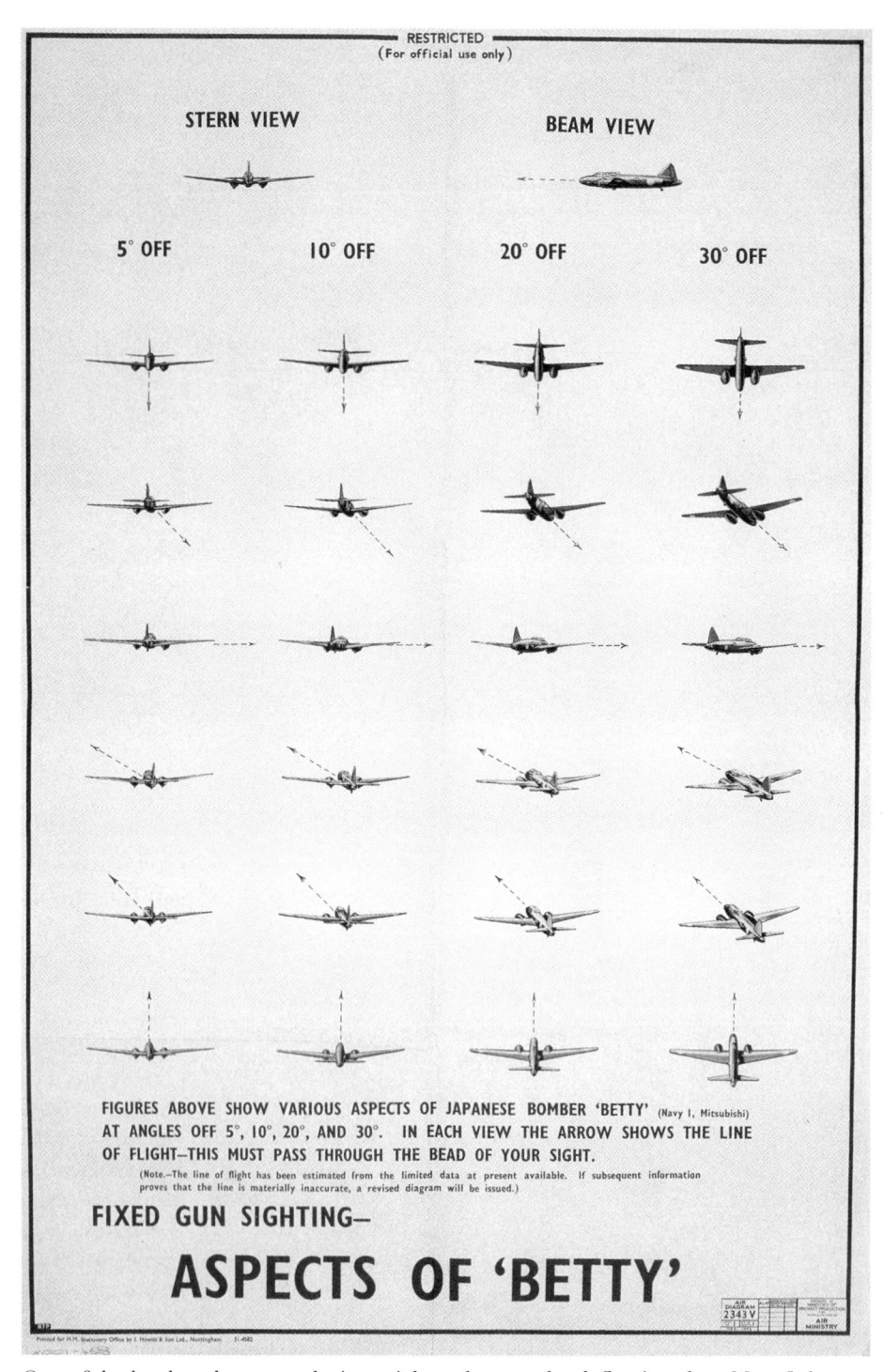

One of the hardest shots to make in aerial combat was the deflection shot. Most fighter pilots found it extremely difficult, and only the best mastered the art. To shoot at a target with high deflection, the pilot first had to position his fighter in the right part of the sky. This chart, "Aspects of Betty," was designed to help Fleet Air Arm and RAF pilots quickly recognize the angle of deflection when approaching a target. (Author's Collection)

A Fleet Air Arm Corsair pours on the power for a go-around and torque stalls, slamming into the crash barrier aboard the HMS *Illustrious*. During World War II, more naval aircraft were lost due to landing and takeoff accidents than were destroyed in combat. (Frank Mitchell via Howard J. Mitchell)

When the British Pacific Fleet moved into the Pacific to join its American cousins, it had to adopt new markings. Here, a Corsair Mk II from 1834 NAS clearly shows the new white bars and white center circle roundels, designed to be similar to the markings that the U.S. Navy used. (Andrew Thomas)

The Seafire Mk III was not equipped with hydraulic-powered folding wings. This photo reveals the manpower required to get a Seafire belonging to 38 Naval Fighter Wing ready for flight, June 1945. (Author's Collection)

Mid-1945. A Seafire Mk III warms up its engine aboard HMS *Implacable*. The drop-tank installation can be clearly seen; it doubled the Seafire's range. In the Pacific Theater, Seafires claimed fifteen Zero-sens destroyed during 1945. (Author's Collection)

Seafire IIIs from 801 and 880 Naval Air Squadrons run up their engines on the deck of HMS *Implacable*, early April 1945. To increase their anemic range, these Seafires are equipped with ex–Curtiss P-40 drop tanks. (Author's Collection)

An all-British affair as Seafires from 894 NAS and Fireflys of 1772 NAS are ready to launch on another strike against Japanese targets, HMS *Indefatigable*. (Author's Collection)

A Corsair Mk II White-Y13x goes nose down after hitting the crash barrier. Of the eighteen FAA squadrons equipped with the type, eight saw combat. FAA Corsair pilots were credited with 52.5 aerial victories. (Author's Collection)

British Royal Navy Aircraft Carriers

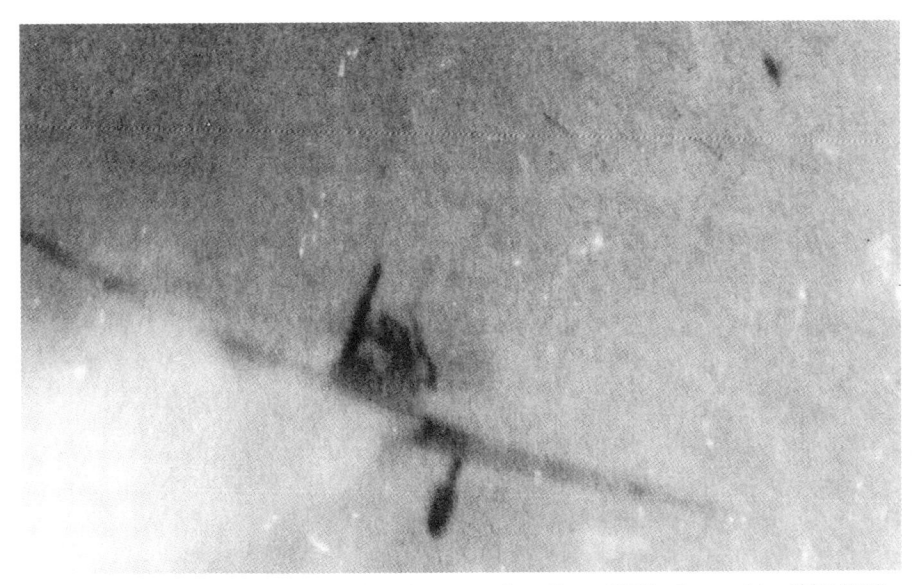

Gun camera image of one of the four Japanese kamikaze Ki-51s downed by 1770 NAS Fireflies on April 12, 1945. (Author's Collection)

On May 5, 1945, a Zero-sen carrying a 250-kilogram bomb struck HMS *Formidable*. The explosion was devastating, with eleven aircraft destroyed, eight sailors killed, and fifty-one wounded. The *Formidable*, however, was saved by its armored deck. Speed was reduced to 18 knots, and the carrier was out of action for just five hours. (Author's Collection)

In early March 1945, the British Pacific Fleet made ready for its part in the invasion of Okinawa, code-named Iceberg. Redesignated as Task Force 57, its four carriers were given the job of neutralizing airfields in the Sakishima Gunto archipelago. Here, Avengers pound Hirara Airfield on Miyako in early April. (Frank Mitchell via Howard J. Mitchell)

On April 13, 1945, Avengers from HMS *Victorious* attacked Shinchiku Airfield on Taiwan. The bomb damage is clearly evident. Because Task Force 57 had no night-bombing capability, the Japanese could easily repair their runways overnight. (Frank Mitchell via Howard J. Mitchell)

Fireflies of 1770 NAS, escorted by Seafires from 887 and 894 NAS from HMS *Indefatigable*, head for another strike on Japanese targets near Tokyo, July 1945. Equipped with drop tanks, the Seafire now had a useful range of four hundred miles, giving it the ability to provide escort to targets in Japan. (Matthew Willis)

Carrier operations during World War II were inherently dangerous. Many aircraft and highly trained pilots were lost while trying to land a high-performance aircraft on a narrow, moving steel deck. Here, one Corsair tries to catch a wire aboard the HMS *Illustrious* as another is caught in the former's prop wash, stalls out, and crashes. (Matthew Willis)

A gun camera still captures the image of a Yokosuka D4Y3 "Judy" as it plunges toward HMS *Illustrious* on April 6, 1945. Diving out of the clouds, the Judy was visible for just eleven seconds before it hit the water short of its target. (Frank Mitchell via Howard J. Mitchell)

On April 1, 1945, the HMS *Victorious* had a near-miss experience with a determined kamikaze. The starboard wing of the "Jill" or "Zeke" struck the port edge of the flight deck, causing the plane to cartwheel into the sea on the port side. The resulting bomb explosion threw tons of water, petrol, and aircraft fragments onto the flight deck. Directly above the carrier is an aircraft that appears to be a Corsair. (Author's Collection)

Seafire Mk III NN 212 catches the crash barrier aboard HMS *Indefatigable*. This was the aircraft Sub-Lt. Michael P. Murphy flew on the last day of the war and obtained his only two aerial victories. Before that he saw action off the Sakishima Gunto Islands during Operation Iceberg I and II in the spring of 1945. (Author's Collection)

Some of the Fleet Air Arm's best. These pilots were involved in the Royal Navy's last air combat of the war. They are (left to right): Sub-Lts. Don Duncan, Randy Kay, "Spud" Murphy, Vic Lowden, Ted Gavin, and "Taffy" Williams, all from 24 Wing HMS *Indefatigable*. In total, they were credited with seven Zero-sens shot down on August 15, 1945. (Via Andrew Thomas)

CHAPTER 3

GERMAN, FRENCH, AND ITALIAN AIRCRAFT CARRIERS

Germany, Italy, and France were the only other nations to build or attempt to complete their own aircraft carriers prior to the outbreak of World War II. France completed the carrier *Bearn* in 1920, with Germany launching the KMS *Graf Zeppelin* on December 8, 1938. Italy began work on its carrier, the *Aqulia*, in July 1941. Pictured here is the launch of the *Graf Zeppelin*. After launch, it was towed to the "equipping pier," where outfitting of the ship's superstructure weapons, catapults, arresting gear, and other machinery and equipment began. (U.S. Naval Historical Center)

The KMS *Graf Zeppelin* was designed to carry twelve modified Bf 109Es, designated Bf 109T, and twenty-two modified Ju 87Es for carrier operations. Each aircraft was equipped with an arrester hook and longer-range radios. A Bf 109 E-0 "GH+NT" with an arrester hook is shown to Ernst Udet, chief of the Technical Office, during his visit to Travemünde in 1940. Note the unusual position of the Werknummer on the rudder. (Francis Marshall)

Bf 109T Werknummer 7743 "RB+OP" photographed on the airfield at Waldau. The first Bf 109T-1 (W.Nr. 7728/RB+OA) rolled out of the Fieseler factory in January 1941. The big difference between the Bf 109E and T version was its larger glider type wing. 63 Bf 109Ts were built but never used on the *Graf Zeppelin*. With a larger wing and more powerful DB 601N engine, the Bf 109Ts were assigned to the narrow and confined airfields found in Norway. (Francis Marshall)

The Arado 197 was an early design for a single-seat German carrier fighter. The Arado 197-V3, seen here, was the third prototype built. First built in 1937, it was completely outclassed by the modified Bf 109 and did not see production. (U.S. Naval Historical Center)

By November 1942 Hitler had lost all faith in the Kriegsmarine's heavy surface battleships and remaining cruisers. With little or no success to show for their efforts, Hitler ordered all major fleet units "paid off" and their guns mounted in the "Atlantic Wall." The fate of the *Graf Zeppelin* had been sealed. The *Graf Zeppelin* is pictured here in 1947. (U.S. Naval Historical Center)

The obvious choice for the *Graf Zeppelin*'s dive-bomber requirements was the Junkers Ju-87 Stuka. This Ju-87C is one of four Ju-87Bs modified for carrier operations. It's equipped with folding wings, arresting hook, catapult cradle attachment points, jettisonable landing gear, a two-man dinghy, and underwing flotation bags. (Author's Collection)

The winning multirole design for a torpedo, reconnaissance patrol aircraft, was Fieseler's excellent Fi 167A. Imbued with Fieseler's innovative short takeoff and landing (STOL) capabilities, the type had excellent slow-speed handling characteristics. (Eddie Nielinger)

Commissioned in 1927, the French FNS *Bearn* was the only other Allied carrier in service at the beginning of the war. After a brief spell of operational duty, it was used to ferry aircraft between the United States and France until the French surrender in June 1940, after which it lay inactive in Martinique for three years. Like many of the carriers built in the late 1920s and 1930s, it was armed for surface warfare and was equipped with four torpedo tubes. Other armament consisted of eight single 6.1-inch guns, six single 75mm guns, and eight single 37mm guns. On board were forty aircraft, twenty-five operational. (U.S. Naval Historical Center)

The aircraft carrier *Aquila* began its life as the Genoa-based *Navigazione Generale Italiana* line's 32,583-ton liner *Roma* in 1940. Like the German *Graf Zeppelin*, the *Aquila* was never completed. Its aircraft complement was to be fifty-one modified Reggiane Re.2001s in the fighter/bomber/torpedo bomber role. (Ryan Noppen)

German, French, and Italian Aircraft Carriers

After five RAF bombing raids on Genoa and the Ansaldo yards between October 22 and November 16, 1942, the *Aquila* was taken out of drydock and moved to a dock in the yard. Heavy camouflage netting was applied to make it look from the air like it was part of the pier. (Ryan Noppen)

CHAPTER 4

JAPANESE AIRCRAFT CARRIERS

Yokosuka B4Y1 Type 96 Carrier attack bomber. This type was used during the early stages of the Sino-Japanese War. The B4Y1 could carry a 1,764-pound torpedo or 1,102 pounds of bombs. (NARA)

The Aichi D1A Type 96 dive-bomber. Based on the German Heinkel He 50, the D1A could carry a single 551-pound bomb and two 66-pound bombs. (NARA)

Hosho, launched in November 1921, was laid down as a mixed seaplane carrier/aircraft carrier employing both seaplanes and deck-launched aircraft. Modified during construction, it was completed as a full-deck aircraft carrier based on a light cruiser hull. *Hosho* could carry nineteen aircraft. (Author's Collection)

In late 1923 work on the carrier *Kaga* began, based on the hull of the incomplete battle cruiser *Amagi*. The multilevel flight-deck arrangement proved impractical. Aircraft can be seen on the forward lower flight deck. For surface engagements, the *Kaga* was armed with two 8-inch gun turrets just below the main flight deck. They were removed during her 1933–1934 modernization. (Author's Collection)

The most successful Japanese light carrier conversions were the Shoho class. Both ships, *Shoho* (Happy Phoenix) and *Zuiho* (Lucky Phoenix), possessed adequate speed and a useful number of aircraft. The ship was armed with four Type 89 mounts and just four triple 25mm cannon mounts. It could carry thirty aircraft. (Author's Collection)

The *Kaga* during high-speed trial runs was capable of 28 knots. The *Kaga* was originally built with three flight decks, as clearly seen in this photograph. It was modernized between 1934 and 1935 and emerged with a single longer upper flight deck. (Author's Collection)

The carrier *Akagi* with three A6M2 Zero-sen fighters at sea during the summer of 1941. In April 1941 the First Air Fleet was created, called the *Kido Butai* (Striking Force). This brought all the IJN's fleet carriers into a single formation. Three carrier divisions made up the *Kido Butai*: the first with *Akagi* and *Kaga*, the second composed of *Soryu* and *Hiryu*, and the third with the newly completed *Shokaku* and *Zuikaku*. The *Kido Butai* would fight as a multicarrier formation. (NARA)

Hiryu (Flying Dagon) running speed trials on April 28, 1939. *Hiryu* epitomized Japanese carrier design philosophy with a relatively large aircraft capacity on a fast, light hull. A total of fifty-seven aircraft were carried, with another sixteen in reserve. *Hiryu* had a maximum speed of 34 knots with a displacement of 17,400 tons. (NARA)

Japanese Aircraft Carriers

The *Kaga* at sea following its 1934–1936 modernization. *Kaga* could carry seventy-two aircraft. *Kaga* stored 154,000 gallons of avgas compared to the USS *Lexington*'s 132,000 gallons. Converted from a battleship hull, *Kaga* possessed the lowest speed of any Japanese fleet carrier, only 27.5 knots. (U.S. Naval Historical Center)

Hiryu in port. Note the 5-inch guns on the port forward quarter and 25mm gun mounts on the bow and along the port side. During the Battle of Midway, it embarked an air group of twenty-one Type 0 Zero-sen Fighters, eighteen Aichi D3A1 Type 99 Carrier Bombers, and eighteen Nakajima B5N2 Type 97 Carrier Attack Planes. *Hiryu*'s air group suffered the heaviest losses of the four Japanese carriers at Midway. (U.S. Naval Historical Center)

The carrier *Chiyoda*, Tokyo Bay, December 1943. After the disastrous loss of four carriers during the Battle of Midway, the need for replacement carriers was critical. To speed the process, the high-speed seaplane carriers *Chitose* and *Chiyoda* were converted into carriers. *Chiyoda* was completed in only ten months. Designed for a capacity of thirty aircraft, these ships carried twenty-one A6M5 fighters and nine attack aircraft during the Battle of the Philippine Sea. During the battle the *Chiyoda* was hit by four bombs and was later sunk by U.S. surface forces. (NARA)

The light carrier *Ryuho* (Heavenly Dragon) underway at sea, September 1938. *Ryuho* was the least successful of the five light carriers converted from auxiliary ships. Its slow speed of just 24 knots and small air group sidelined it for second-line duties. It spent most of service life as an aircraft ferry and training vessel. (U.S. Naval Historical Center)

Soryu (Deep Blue Dragon) has the distinction of being the first Japanese fleet carrier designed as such from the keel up. During the Battle of Midway, it embarked twenty-one Zero-sen fighters, sixteen Aichi D3A1 dive-bombers, eighteen B5N2 Type 97 Carrier Attack Planes, and one new Yokosuka D4Y1 "Judy" Type 2 Carrier Bomber earmarked for reconnaissance. (U.S. Naval Historical Center)

Junyo moored at Sasebo, Japan, autumn 1945. *Junyo* was commissioned in May 1942 and saw its first action as part of the Northern Force assigned to occupy two islands in the Aleutians as part of the Midway operation. Aircraft capacity was rated at forty-eight with five in reserve. *Junyo* survived the war and was later scrapped. (U.S. Naval Historical Center)

A Japanese cruiser mounting the 5-inch/40 Type 89 twin turret antiaircraft gun. These dual mounts were standard on board all IJN carriers but one in 1942. It had an effective range of 8,750 yards but had difficulty tracking fast-moving targets and was forced to use barrage fire tactics against incoming attacking planes. (U.S. Naval Historical Center)

The *Kaga*'s stern after its major reconstruction. After just over four years in service, the multilevel flight deck proved impractical. The two lower flight decks were removed, and the main flight deck was extended to 815 feet. A third elevator and small island were added. Aircraft capacity increased to seventy-two plus eighteen reserves. (U.S. Naval Historical Center)

Japanese Aircraft Carriers

The *Ryujo* at speed. When built, the *Ryujo* was heavily armed with six Type 89 5-inch gun mounts and twenty-four 12.7mm machine guns. Two of the 5-inch gun turrets were removed in *Ryujo*'s first refit. By the outbreak of the Pacific War, the machine guns had been replaced with twenty-two 25mm guns in a mix of double and triple mounts. *Ryujo* was sunk by four bombs and one torpedo during the Battle of the Eastern Solomons. (U.S. Naval Historical Center)

The *Zuikaku* (Flying Crane) was essentially an upgraded *Hiryu* but was one hundred feet longer and eighty-five hundred tons heavier. Capable of carrying seventy-two aircraft and twelve reserves, it was armed with eight 5-inch Type 89 twin turrets and twelve 25mm cannon triple mounts. Japanese antiaircraft defenses proved inferior in contrast to American antiaircraft gunnery and was not a factor in the carrier battles of 1942. (U.S. Naval Historical Center)

Unryu (Heaven-bound Dragon Riding the Clouds). As war approached, the Imperial Navy took steps to construct a large number of fleet carriers. Between 1941 and 1942, six carriers were ordered, but only three—*Unryu*, *Amagi*, and *Katsuragi*—were completed. Commissioned in August 1944, *Unryu* had no air group and was used as a cargo vessel. On December 19, 1944, it was torpedoed by the submarine USS *Redfish*, and it sank. (U.S. Naval Historical Center)

Katsuragi (A mountain near Osaka). *Katsuragi* was commissioned into service in October 1944 but did not leave home waters because of fuel, aircraft, and aircrew shortages. (U.S. Naval Historical Center)

Taiho (Great Phoenix) pictured after its arrival at Tawi Tawi anchorage in May 1944. On deck are a number of A6M5 fighters and Nakajima B6N "Jill" attack aircraft. This ship was the first Japanese carrier designed to receive battle damage and continue fighting. An armored flight deck was incorporated, designed to withstand 1,000-pound bomb hits. The *Taiho*'s career was short. On May 19, 1944, it was hit by a single torpedo from the U.S. submarine *Albacore*. The damage from the torpedo and poor damage control by ship's crew caused aviation fuel vapor to spread throughout the ship, and six hours later a huge explosion rocked the ship, sending it to the bottom. (U.S. Naval Historical Center)

Japanese Aircraft Carriers

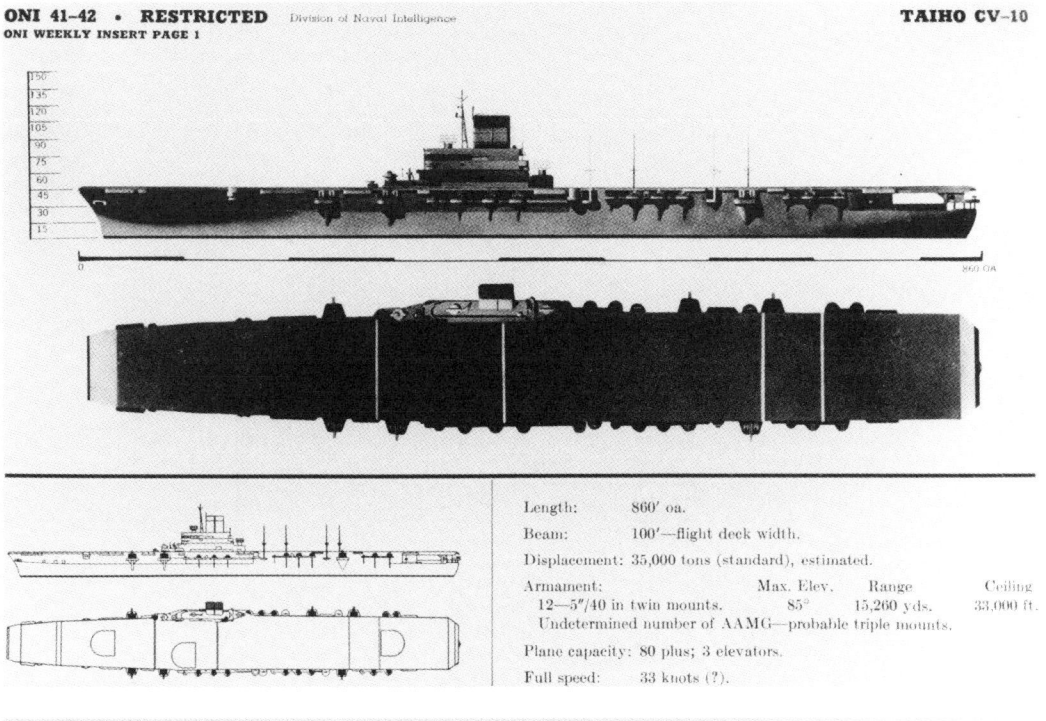

U.S. Navy ship recognition profiles of the Japanese carrier *Taiho*. Japanese carrier production during the war was no match for the industrial might of the United States. Just five fleet carriers were completed compared to seventeen Essex-class carriers; to the 5 escort carriers built, the U.S. answered with 125. (U.S. Naval Historical Center)

Pacific Ocean, November 1941. Japanese ships are heading toward Pearl Harbor. This photograph was taken from the superstructure of the carrier *Zuikaku*. The vessel visible in the background is *Kaga*. (Author's Collection)

An A6M2 Zero-sen Type 21 is seen lashed to the flight deck of IJN carrier *Akagi* in Hitokappu Bay, the Kure Islands, late November 1941. The Japanese fleet gathered here prior to heading south to attack the U.S. Fleet at Pearl Harbor. (Author's Collection)

Dawn, December 7, 1941. The Japanese attack on Pearl Harbor. An A6M2 Zero-sen prepares for takeoff. Behind it are Aichi "Val" dive-bombers. This photograph reportedly shows the second wave ready for launch. All six of Japan's first-line aircraft carriers—*Akagi, Kaga, Soryu, Hiryu, Shokaku,* and *Zuikaku*—were assigned to the mission. With more than 420 embarked planes, these ships constituted by far the most powerful carrier task force ever assembled. (U.S. Naval Historical Center)

Aichi D3A1 Type 99 Carrier Bombers "Val" prepare to take off from an aircraft carrier during the morning of December 7, 1941. Ship in the background is the carrier *Soryu*. Although inferior to the American SBD Dauntless in terms of bomb load and survivability, the Val sank more Allied warship tonnage than any other Axis aircraft during World War II. It was responsible for the sinking of the first Allied aircraft carrier, HMS *Hermes*, in April 1942. (U.S. Naval Historical Center)

Japanese Nakajima B5N2 Type 97 Carrier Attack Plane "Kate" takes off from the aircraft carrier *Shokaku* en route to attack Pearl Harbor. During the attack, the Kate was used as both a torpedo bomber and horizontal bomber armed with a single 800 kg Type 99 No 80 Mk 5 armor-piercing bomb. (U.S. Naval Historical Center)

An A6M2 Zero-sen fighter on the aircraft carrier *Akagi* prior to the Pearl Harbor attack mission. The Zero-sen's drop tank—one of the first to be regularly carried on a fighter—helped give the aircraft phenomenal range for a single-engine fighter. During the Pearl Harbor attack, seventy-nine Zero-sens flew fighter escort and strafing missions. (U.S. Naval Historical Center)

With deck crew cheering, an A6M2 Zero-sen takes off bound for Pearl Harbor. The Zero-sen was the most maneuverable carrier-based fighter of the Pacific campaign thanks to its large wing area and generously proportioned ailerons. (U.S. Naval Historical Center)

An Aichi D3A1 "Val" of the second wave, probably from *Kaga*, pulls up after its dive over the harbor. Vals were assigned both ship and airfield targets. Japanese losses during Pearl Harbor amounted to twenty-nine aircraft shot down. Vals accounted for fifteen of that number, with six others so badly damaged that they were pushed overboard. (U.S. Naval Historical Center)

Facing page bottom: A6M2 Zero-sen with engines running prepares to take off aboard the carrier *Akagi* on December 7, 1941. The A6M2 was considered to be heavily armed, but its two-wing mounted Type 99-1 20mm cannons had some major drawbacks. With just sixty rounds per gun, the Zero-sen pilots had just ten seconds worth of firing. Secondary armament consisted of two Type 97 7.7mm machine guns with five hundred rounds per gun. (U.S. Naval Historical Center)

An A6M2 Zero-sen aboard the carrier *Akagi*, December 7, 1941. On the morning of the Pearl Harbor attack, the six carriers maintained a fighter combat air patrol (CAP) over the fleet. Each carrier contributed nine Zero-sens for fleet air defense—three on CAP, three ready on deck for immediate launch, and three on fifteen-minute readiness. (Author's Collection)

With bomb racks empty, two of *Zuikaku*'s "Kates" depart from Trincomalee harbor having just bombed the port and airfield on April 9, 1942. Shortly after 6 a.m. on April 9, five carriers of the IJN (*Akagi, Soryu, Hiryu, Shokaku,* and *Zuikaku*) of the 1st Koku Sentai Fleet launched B5N2s, escorted by A6Ms, one hundred miles east of Trincomalee, home to the Royal Navy dockyard and the RAF airfield at China Bay. (Author's Collection)

A deck crewman takes a break resting on the main wheel of an A6M2 Zero-sen aboard *Akagi* sometime in 1942. *Akagi* could carry ninety-one aircraft (sixty-three operational) and had a maximum speed of 31 knots. (Author's Collection)

Japanese Aircraft Carriers

The *Kido Butai* during the Indian Ocean operation of April 1942. This photo clearly shows the power of this formation. *Akagi* is leading the column that includes, in order, *Soryu*, *Hiryu*, all four Kongo-class battleships, and the two Shokaku-class carriers. By April the IJN carrier force had reached the zenith of its success. From December 7 to April 9, Japanese naval air power had sunk five U.S. battleships, one British battleship, and one battle cruiser (by land-based torpedo bombers), the British carrier *Hermes*, along with two heavy cruisers and two destroyers. (U.S. Naval Historical Center)

The Japanese light carrier *Shoho* is torpedoed during attacks by U.S. Navy carrier aircraft in the late morning of May 7, 1942, during the Battle of the Coral Sea. *Shoho* was the first carrier sunk by U.S. carrier aircraft. TDB-1 Devastators from *Yorktown* and *Lexington* claimed nineteen hits from the twenty-two torpedoes dropped, but the accepted figure is seven. Thirteen bombs hit were also registered. (U.S. Naval Historical Center)

Japanese Aircraft Carriers

Shokaku under attack during the Battle of the Coral Sea, May 8, 1942. SBDs from *Lexington* and *Yorktown* scored three hits on the twenty-thousand-ton carrier, causing heavy damage. Losses on the American side included the carrier *Lexington*, destroyer *Sims*, fleet oiler *Neosho*, the carrier *Yorktown* damaged along with fifty-six carrier aircraft (sixteen fighters, twenty-seven dive-bombers, and thirteen torpedo planes). The Japanese lost the light carrier *Shoho*, *Shokaku* damaged, and eighty-five carrier aircraft (twenty-five fighters, twenty-six carrier bombers, and thirty-four carrier attack planes). (U.S. Naval Historical Center)

Often cited as a B5N2 Type 97 "Kate" taking off for the Pearl Harbor attack, this is, in fact, a still image taken from the Japanese motion picture *Hawai Mare Oki Kaisen* (The War at Sea from Hawaii to Malaya) produced in 1942. The B5N2 is armed with a dummy Type 91 aerial torpedo. The nose cone is clearly dented. (U.S. Naval Historical Center)

A B5N2 "Kate" Carrier Attack Plane recovering aboard *Shokaku*. Note the trailing destroyer acting as a plane guard. Compared to the U.S. Devastator torpedo bomber, the Kate was far superior in the key areas of speed, range, and rate of climb. It was also equipped with the deadly and reliable Type 91 torpedo. This allowed for higher dropping altitudes and higher attack speeds, limiting its exposure to antiaircraft fire. (U.S. Naval Historical Center)

Japanese Aircraft Carriers

The Japanese carrier *Soryu* making a high-speed turn during the Battle of Midway, June 3, 1942. During the battle it was hit by three 1,000-pound bombs from the dive-bombers of U.S. Navy squadron VB-3 from the USS *Yorktown*. The three bombs ripped through the flight deck, igniting an inferno the Japanese had no hope of extinguishing, and it sank shortly thereafter. (Author's Collection)

The carrier *Hiryu* suffered four bomb hits (for the loss of three U.S. Navy SBDs) during the Battle of Midway and was left a burning wreck, sinking on June 5. All four Japanese fleet carriers assigned to the battle were sunk along with all their aircraft (247). The string of Japanese victories in 1942 had come to an end. (U.S. Naval Historical Center)

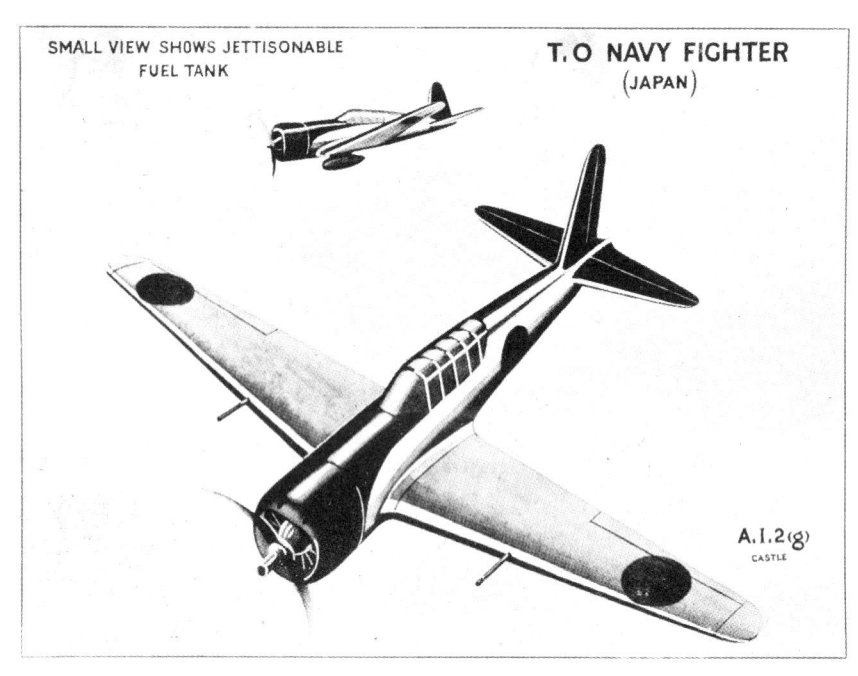

The lack of Allied information on the A6M Zero-sen prewar is clear in this early British Air Intelligence 2(g) drawing purportedly of the Japanese fighter. It bears a strong resemblance to the Vultee P-66 Vanguard, 129 of which were supplied to the Chinese in 1940. (U.S. Naval Historical Center)

On board *Shokaku* as it prepares to launch aircraft in the morning of October 26, 1942, during the Battle of the Santa Cruz Islands. This would be the final carrier battle of 1942. The Americans would lose the carrier USS *Hornet* and eighty aircraft. The Japanese lost ninety-eight carrier aircraft, and the carriers *Shokaku* and *Zuiho* were damaged. At the end of 1942, the Japanese carrier force still possessed five flight decks—*Shokaku, Zuikaku, Junyo, Hiyo,* and *Zuiho*—but sufficient aircraft and aviators to man them were nonexistent. The Americans had just one operational carrier, the USS *Saratoga*. (U.S. Naval Historical Center)

Captured B5N2 "Kate" equipped with the Type H6 airborne air-to-surface radar. The antennae can be seen clearly along the red fuselage and leading edge of the wing. Airborne radar gave both sides the ability to strike at night and in bad weather. (U.S. Naval Historical Center)

Battle of the Philippine Sea, June 1944. The Japanese carriers *Taiho, Shokaku, Zuikaku, Junyo, Hiyo, Ryuho, Chitose, Chiyoda,* and *Zuiho* would launch 245 aircraft for the first strike of the day against the American carrier task force. It would be the largest number of carrier-based aircraft sent against the U.S. Pacific Fleet during the war. Here the Japanese aircraft carrier *Zuikaku* (center) and two destroyers maneuvering while under attack by U.S. Navy carrier aircraft during the late afternoon of June 20, 1944. *Zuikaku* was hit by several bombs during these attacks but survived. (U.S. Naval Historical Center)

Battle of Leyte Gulf, October 1944. This would be the IJN's final carrier action of the war. With just 116 embarked on four carriers, this force was primarily used as a decoy to draw away U.S. carrier aircraft from the Third and Seventh Fleets and let the nine Japanese battleships, twenty cruisers, and more than thirty-five destroyers attack the American invasion fleet in Leyte Gulf. Japanese aircraft carrier *Zuiho* still underway after several hits by planes from Task Force 38 during the battle off Cape Engaño, October 25, 1944. (U.S. Naval Historical Center)

Japanese Aircraft Carriers

Japanese Chitose-class CVL under attack by U.S. Task Force 38 aircraft during the battle off Cape Engaño, October 25, 1944. The ship may be the light carrier *Zuiho*. It suffered two torpedo hits, several bomb hits, and innumerable near misses and later sank. (U.S. Naval Historical Center)

Battle of the Philippine Sea, June 1944. Japanese carrier *Chiyoda* is hit aft and near-missed several times during air attacks by TF-58 planes on June 20. *Chiyoda* survived the battle only to be sunk by four bombs and U.S. naval gunfire during the Battle of Leyte Gulf, October 25, 1944. (U.S. Naval Historical Center)

Japanese Aircraft Carriers 143

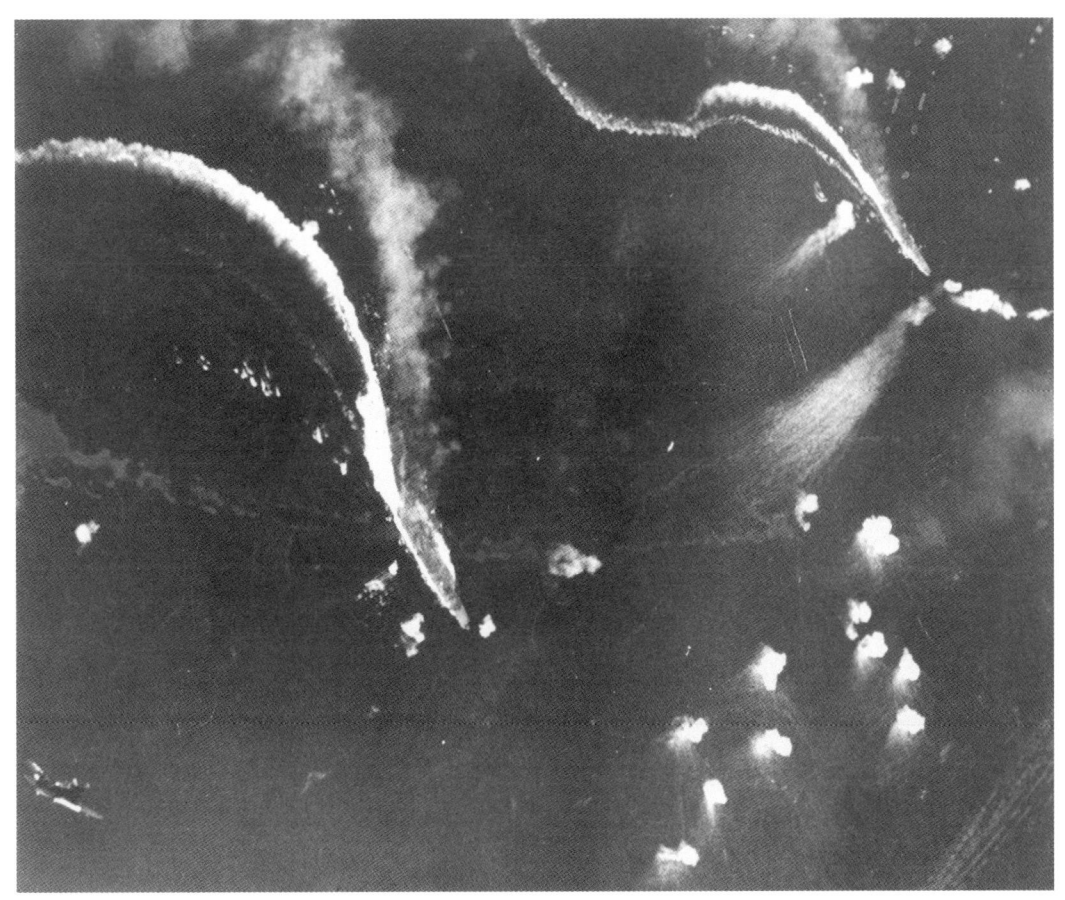

This remarkable photograph shows the Japanese carriers *Zuikaku* (left center) and *Zuiho* under attack by U.S. Navy dive-bombers, October 25, 1944. Both ships appear to be making good speed, indicating that this photo was taken relatively early in the action. Both carriers are emitting heavy smoke. Note the heavy concentration of bursting antiaircraft fire at lower right and a SB2C Helldiver with dive flaps open diving toward *Zuikaku*. It would be hit by seven torpedoes and take nine bomb hits before sinking. (U.S. Naval Historical Center)

Japanese Aichi D3A2 "Vals" taxi out for a kamikaze mission on the outskirts of Manila, Philippines, 1944. The Val was one of the most prevalent kamikazes and was usually armed with a single 551-pound Type 99 bomb on its centerline rack. The U.S. Navy and its Allies had sixty-six ships or craft sunk or never repaired and almost four hundred damaged in some measure by kamikaze attack. (U.S. Naval Historical Center)

The Nakajima B5N2 "Kate" was used in many roles—torpedo bomber, horizontal bomber, search and patrol, and as an antisubmarine patrol aircraft. While on an ASW patrol near the Caroline Islands, this late-war B5N2 fell victim to a U.S. Navy Consolidated PB4Y-1 Liberator of VB-109, June 6, 1944. This B5N2 crashed into the water and exploded simultaneously with the release of its depth bombs. (U.S. Naval Historical Center)

The Japanese battleship *Ise* underway off Sata Point, August 24, 1943, after conversion to a hybrid aircraft carrier. To partially compensate for the loss of carrier strength at Midway, the Navy Aircraft Department began plans to convert the ISE-class battleships to full-sized carriers, each carrying fifty-four planes. This concept was abandoned due to lack of time and resources and the hybrid battleship/carriers concept was adopted. (U.S. Naval Historical Center)

Japanese Aircraft Carriers

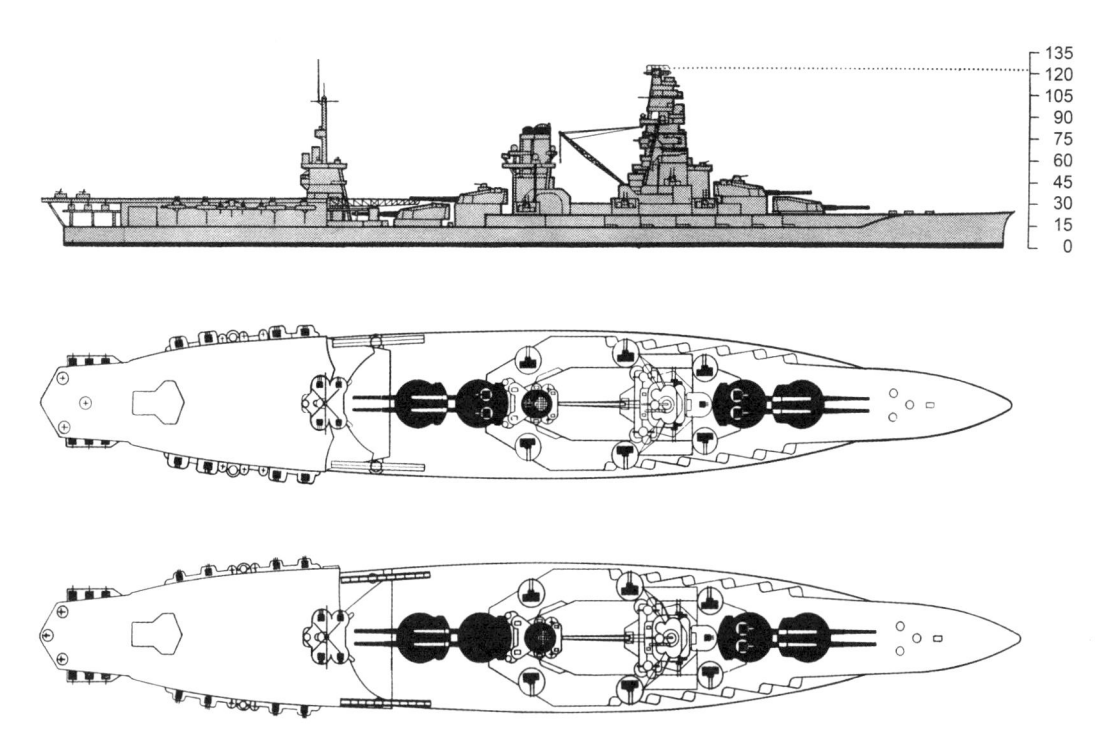

Recognition profile of the hybrid battleship/carrier *Ise*. *Ise* was modified to carry twenty-two aircraft. The concept of operations called for the modified *Ise* to accompany the Main Carrier Striking Force and catapult their complement of Yokosuka D4Y2 Suisei "Judy" dive-bombers and Aichi E16A Zuiun "Paul" seaplanes, both capable of diving attacks. The aircraft cannot take off from or land on the small flight deck; rather, they are catapult-launched and land either on conventional carriers or land bases. (Author's Collection)

Smoke from the Japanese battleship/carrier *Ise*'s antiaircraft and main forward guns smothers the ship as SB2C Helldivers from Air Group 15 press home their attacks. During battle off Cape Engaño, October 25, 1944, *Ise* suffered minor damage. (U.S. Naval Historical Center)

Battle off Cape Engaño, October 25, 1944. Crewmembers of the listing Japanese aircraft carrier *Zuikaku* throwing explosives over the side after being damaged by U.S. carrier aircraft. (U.S. Naval Historical Center)

Aichi D3A2 "Vals" ready for takeoff. The new D3A2 was only a slight improvement on the D3A1 version. When the D4Y Carrier Bomber ("Judy") was introduced in 1943 to replace the improved Aichi D3A2, the Val was assigned to secondary roles. From the autumn of 1944, land-based Vals were increasingly used as kamikaze aircraft, and in 1945 those examples previously assigned to training duties were brought back into frontline service to bolster the number of kamikaze aircraft. (U.S. Naval Historical Center)

On November 5, 1943, the USS *Saratoga* and light carrier USS *Princeton* raided the Japanese stronghold at Rabaul. Ninety-seven aircraft took part in the raid. Five Japanese heavy cruisers were damaged in the attack. This A6M5 Zero-sen was one of the many Japanese aircraft destroyed on the ground during the strike. (navsource.org)

Battle off Cape Engaño, October 25, 1944. Japanese aircraft carrier *Zuikaku* under attack at about 2 p.m., approximately at the end of the day's third attack on the Japanese force. *Zuikaku* appears to be listing but is still underway. Earlier in the day, at 11:55 a.m., *Zuikaku* launched twenty-nine aircraft in what would be the last offensive strike generated by a Japanese carrier during the war. (U.S. Naval Historical Center)

Japanese Aircraft Carriers

Japanese aircraft carrier *Zuikaku* underway early in the action on October 25, 1944. Although capable of making good speed, it is making smoke to throw off U.S. Navy torpedo bomber attacks. Note camouflage pattern painted on the flight deck. (U.S. Naval Historical Center)

The carrier *Kasagi* seen here after the war. The *Kasagi* was 84 percent complete when hostilities ended. Like all the other Japanese carriers, either under construction or still afloat in 1945, none would have been capable of offensive operations. Lack of fuel and nonexistent trained aircrew meant they would remain empty shells. (U.S. Naval Historical Center)

Japanese Aircraft Carriers

Aircraft from *Essex* (CV-9) attack two Japanese carriers at Kure Harbor, March 19, 1945. An SB2C Helldiver on the upper right is pulling up from its dive. The carrier at the bottom is the *Amagi*. The smaller carrier is the *Kaiyo*. Like the rest of the Japanese fleet, IJN carriers were sitting targets capable of providing only some local antiaircraft defense. (U.S. Naval Historical Center)

Japanese escort aircraft carrier *Kaiyo* beached in Beppu Bay, Kyushu, Japan, while being scrapped. *Kaiyo* entered fleet service in November 1943 and was used to ferry aircraft and escort convoys throughout 1944. In 1945, it was transferred to the Inland Sea and was used as a target for kamikaze pilot training. After suffering minor damage at Kure in March 1945, it was sunk on July 24, 1945, by U.S. carrier aircraft. (U.S. Naval Historical Center)

The Japanese carrier *Ibuki* lies incomplete at Sasebo, Japan, November 2, 1945. Following the heavy carrier losses suffered in 1942, the *Ibuki* was converted from a heavy cruiser hull into a light carrier. Delays in construction meant that the ship was never completed. (U.S. Naval Historical Center)

Escort carriers proved versatile and dependable. Here the USS *Copahee* (CVE-12) performs a unique task. This photograph shows four of the thirteen Zero-sen fighters, one B5N2 "Kate," and thirty-seven aircraft engines bound for San Diego, California. (NARA)

The Japanese carrier *Junyo*. A member of the ship's residual crew signals an approaching tug from the carrier's flight deck. Taken at Sasebo, Japan, October 19, 1945. *Junyo* was equipped with both Type 21 and Type 13 radar. The Type 21 is the mattress spring antenna forward of the stack. Performance was mediocre, with the ability to detect a group of aircraft at approximately sixty miles and a single aircraft at about forty-five miles. (U.S. Naval Historical Center)

A D4Y1-C "Judy," possibly from the 523rd Kokutai in the Mariana Islands during spring 1944. The D4Y1 was designed to replace the D3A1 "Val" dive-bomber. The Judy was the fastest carrier-borne dive-bomber of the war and one of the most versatile—serving as a light bomber, night fighter, and reconnaissance aircraft. This aircraft is configured for a long-range reconnaissance mission, with single 330-liter drop tanks beneath each wing and a smaller, semi-recessed tank fitted in the bomb bay. (NARA)

In early 1939 the Imperial Naval staff issued a request for a replacement for the B5N2 "Kate." The new specification called for a three-seat carrier-borne torpedo bomber with a top speed of 288mph and a range of 1,151 miles with a 1,760-pound bomb load. The result was the Nakajima B6N2 Tenzan (codenamed "Jill"). The Jill slowly replaced the B5N Kate as the IJNAF's premier carrier-borne torpedo bomber from late 1943. (NARA)

The Japanese carrier *Amagi* was the last IJN flattop sunk in the Pacific War by U.S. Navy aircraft. After suffering light damage from a U.S. carrier aircraft in March, it suffered heavy damage in another raid on July 24 and was finally sunk on July 28, 1945. The Imperial Navy's fleet carrier construction program was no match for the industrial might of the United States. With just five new ships entering service during war, the Americans commissioned 17 Essex-class carriers, 9 Independence-class light carriers, and 129 escort carriers. (U.S. Naval Historical Center)

Japanese Aircraft Carriers

JAPANESE NAVAL AIR STRENGTH, PRODUCTION AND WASTAGE

ANNEX "B" TO U.S.S.B.S. 414 (NAV. NO. 86)

TYPE	ON HAND 1 DEC. 1941	1941 DEC.1941 TO MAR.1942 PRODUCED	1941 DEC.1941 TO MAR.1942 EXPENDED	ON HAND 1 APR. 1942	1942 APR.1942 TO MAR.1943 PRODUCED	1942 APR.1942 TO MAR.1943 EXPENDED	ON HAND 1 APR. 1943	1943 APR.1943 TO MAR.1944 PRODUCED	1943 APR.1943 TO MAR.1944 EXPENDED	ON HAND 1 APR. 1944	1944 APR.1944 TO MAR.1945 PRODUCED	1944 APR.1944 TO MAR.1945 EXPENDED	ON HAND 1 APR. 1945	1945 APR.1945 TO AUG.1945 PRODUCED	1945 APR.1945 TO AUG.1945 EXPENDED	ON HAND 15 AUG. 1945	GRAND TOTAL PRODUCED	GRAND TOTAL EXPENDED
FIGHTERS	660	316	300	676	1747	1590	833	3864	2843	1854	5074	4150	2778	1343	2420	1701	12344	11303
SHIPBOARD ATTACK & BOMBER	330	123	146	307	465	762	10	1820	1191	639	2445	2150	904	456	936	424	5279	5185
LAND ATTACK & BOMBER	240	219	182	277	674	465	486	774	969	291	1661	1436	516	342	640	218	3670	3692
RECONN. AND PATROL	10			10		1	9	27	12	24	334	181	177	225	150	252	586	344
SPECIAL ATTACK (BAKA PLANES)											750		750		70	680	750	70
TRANSPORT	45	18	20	43	99	57	85	78	64	99	179	178	100	59	92	47	413	411
FLOAT RECONN.	270	64	93	241	500	445	296	1045	492	849	851	870	830	85	610	305	2545	2510
FLYING BOATS	55	29	22	62	96	45	113	87	68	132	57	105	84	2	74	12	271	314
TRAINER	510	212	92	630	862	344	1148	2257	695	2710	2840	1260	4290	348	970	3668	6519	3361
TOTAL	2120	981	855	2246	4443	3709	2980	9952	6334	6598	14161	10330	10429	2840	5962	7307	32377	27190

1. NUMBER OF PLANES ON HAND IS TOTAL OF THOSE IN USE AND THOSE IN STORAGE.
2. NUMBER OF PLANES EXPENDED INCLUDE OPERATIONAL LOSSES. IN THE 1945 COLUMN UNDER PLANES EXPENDED, THOSE IN OUTLYING AREAS (EXCEPTING KOREA AND FORMOSA) ARE NOT INCLUDED.

PLATE 86-9

This chart, completed after the war, illustrates the production and loss of Japanese naval aircraft during the Pacific War. The Japanese had planned for a short war; Japan's inability to match American industrial output was well known and feared by some in the Japanese high command. In terms of naval carrier aircraft production, the comparative numbers speak for themselves. Having produced just 12,344 single-seat naval fighters, the Americans were able to answer with a stunning 27,655 F4F/FM-2 Wildcats, F6F Hellcats, and F4U Corsairs. (U.S. Naval Historical Center)

ABOUT THE AUTHOR

Donald Nijboer is a best-selling aviation author/historian/documentary writer-producer and Smithsonian Speaker who lives in Toronto, Canada. He is the author of several aviation titles, including: *The Mighty Eighth—Masters of the Air over Europe 1942-45, SBD Dauntless vs A6M Zero, German Flak Defences vs Allied Heavy Bomber, Flak in World War II, B-29 Superfortress vs Ki 44 Tojo 1945, Fighting Cockpits, Air Combat 1945, Spitfire Mk V vs C.202 Folgore, Gloster Meteor vs V-1 Flying Bomb, Seafire vs A6M Zero, P-38 Lightning vs Ki 61 Tony, Graphic War: The Secret Aviation Drawings and Illustrations of World War II*. He is also the co-author with photographer Dan Patterson of *Cockpit: An Illustrated History of World War II Aircraft Interiors, Gunner: An Illustrated History of World War II Aircraft Turrets and Gun Positions*, and *Cockpits of the Cold War*.